To Dad

For you on your 50th Birthday. a guide for your walks with Hardy as a companion.

Love Mark.

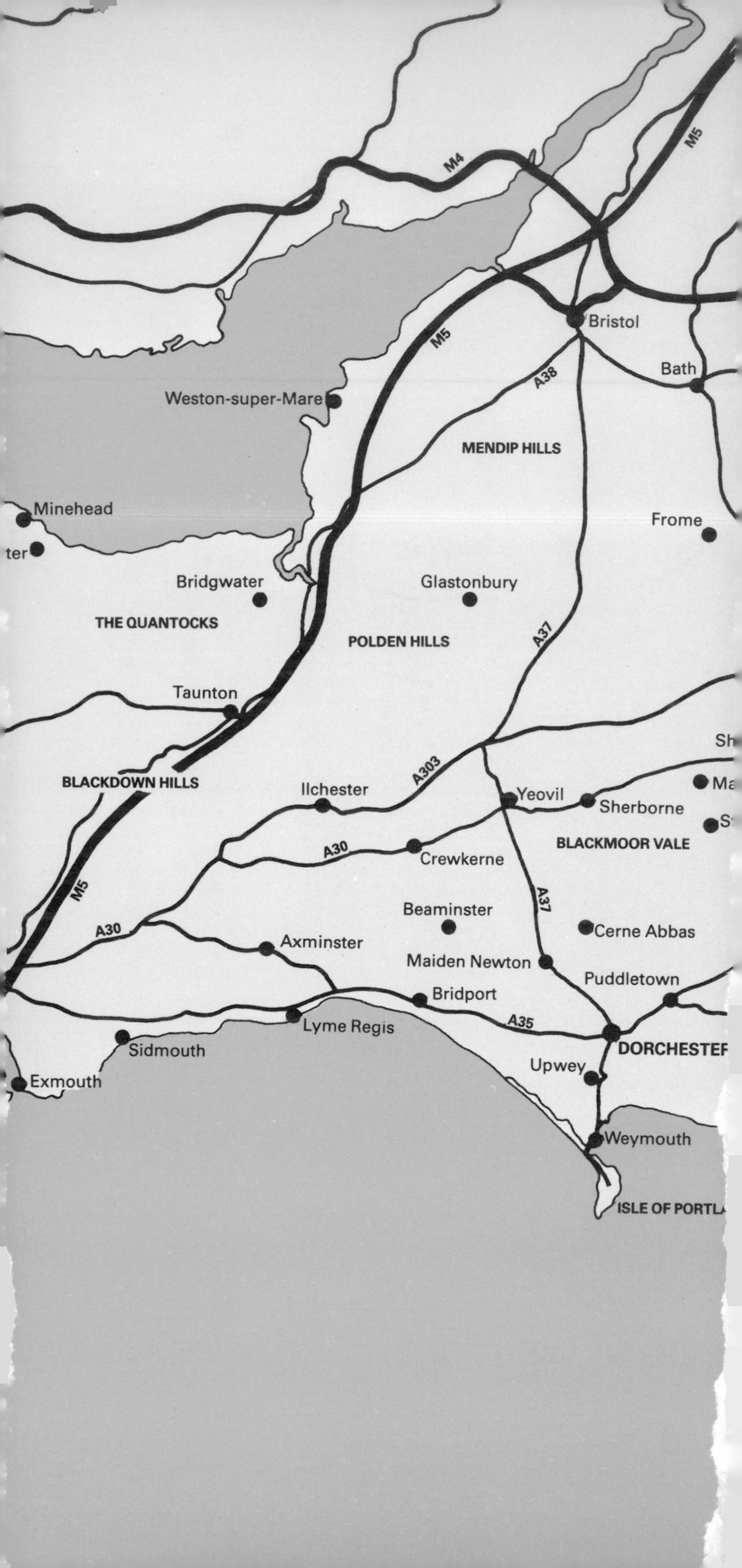
M4
M5
Bristol
Bath
A38
Weston-super-Mare
MENDIP HILLS
Minehead
Frome
Bridgwater
Glastonbury
THE QUANTOCKS
POLDEN HILLS
A37
Taunton
BLACKDOWN HILLS
A303
Ilchester
Yeovil
Sherborne
A30
Crewkerne
BLACKMOOR VALE
Beaminster
Cerne Abbas
Axminster
Maiden Newton
Puddletown
Bridport
A35
Lyme Regis
Sidmouth
DORCHESTER
Upwey
Exmouth
Weymouth

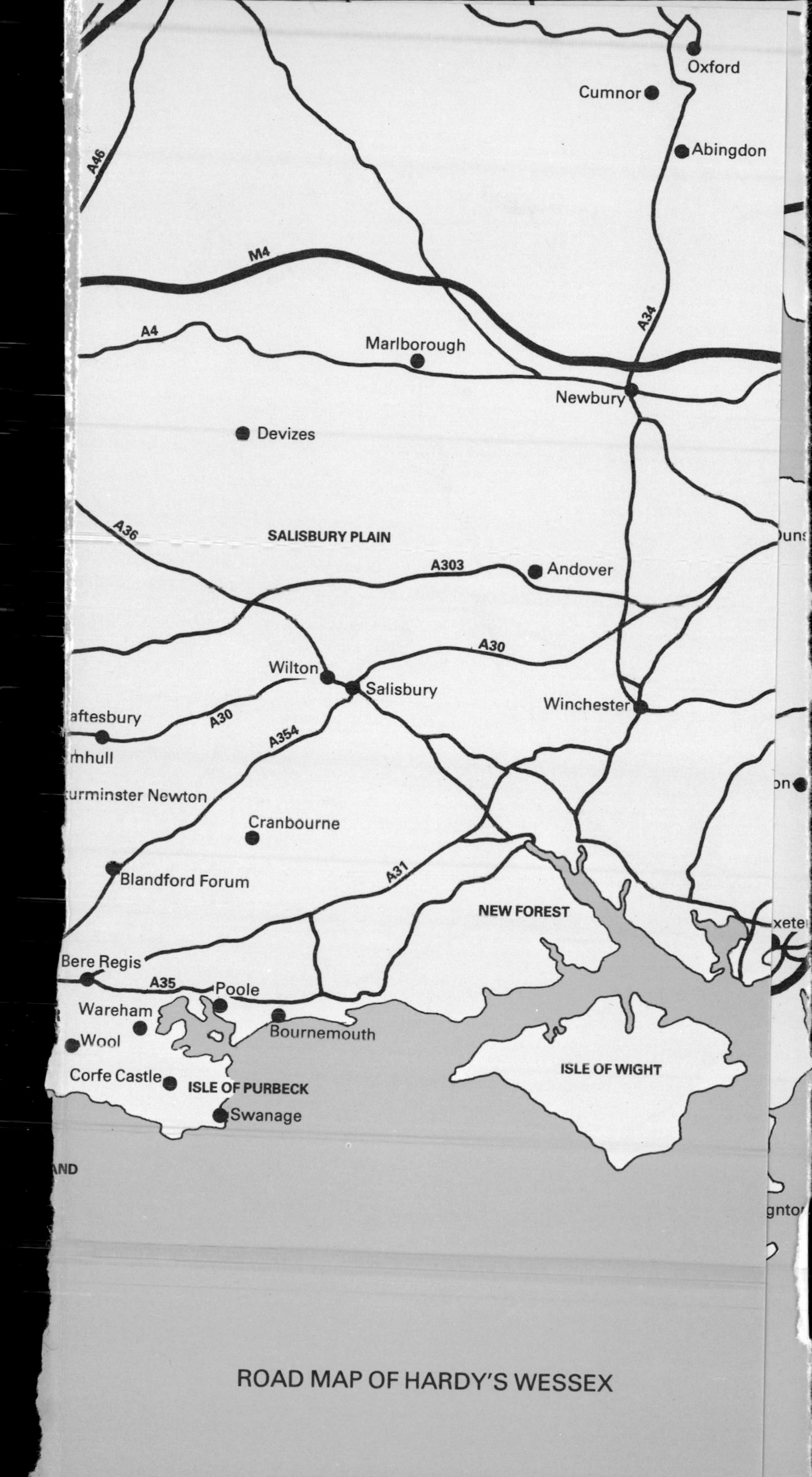

ROAD MAP OF HARDY'S WESSEX

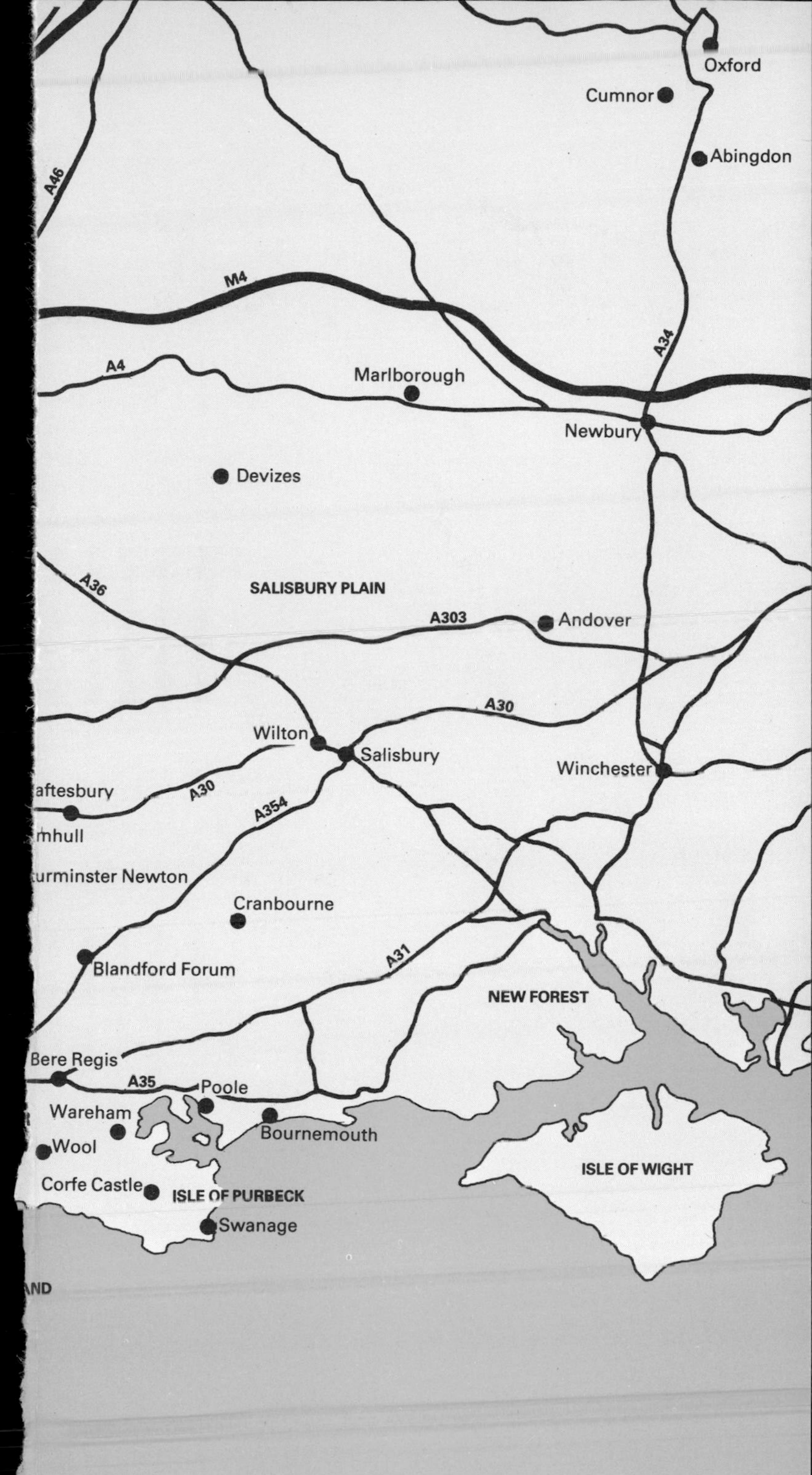

ROAD MAP OF HARDY'S WESSEX

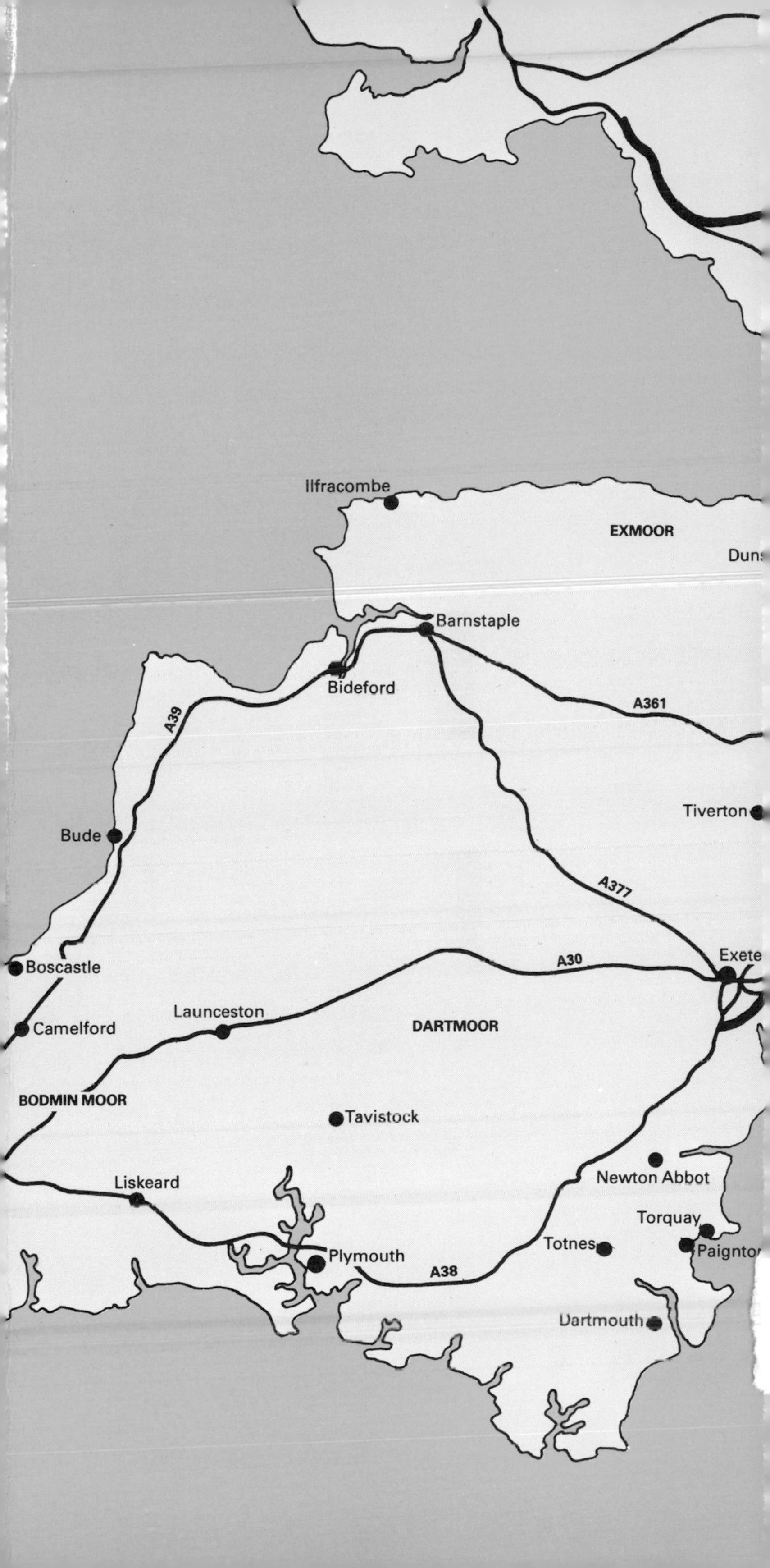

Ilfracombe
EXMOOR
Duns
Barnstaple
Bideford
A361
A39
Tiverton
Bude
A377
Exete
A30
Boscastle
Launceston
Camelford
DARTMOOR
BODMIN MOOR
Tavistock
Newton Abbot
Liskeard
Torquay
Totnes
Plymouth
Paignto
A38
Dartmouth

Penguin Books
The Hardy Guides Volume 1

Hermann Lea was born in 1869 at Thorpe-Le-Soken, Essex, and died three days before his eighty-third birthday, one of the few surviving personal friends of Thomas Hardy. As a young man, Lea became a pupil of Mr Wood Home at Athelhampton Hall to learn farming, but he was more devoted to dogs, horse-riding and tennis. His love of animals prompted him to become a vegetarian and he was known, on occasions, to attack anyone he saw ill-treating an animal.

Keenly interested in natural history, many of the observations he made provided valuable records in that field. His skills lay too in building, bee-keeping, gardening and poultry farming. He was also greatly interested in witchcraft and he wrote several articles on the subject. Lea did a great deal of his writing, including articles for *The Animals' Friend*, in a small wooden house he built in the garden of his house at Higher Bockhampton, which had been the birthplace and home of Hardy.

It was photography, however, that became his most absorbing interest and he was an active member of the Dorset Photographic Club. He planned to supply photographs for an illustrated edition of the Wessex Novels, and Thomas Perkins, the Secretary of the Club, introduced Lea to Hardy in order to discuss the project. The plan proved impossible but, with Hardy's assistance, Lea did capture the Wessex countryside as portrayed in the novels and was invited to have the fruit of his labours – *Thomas Hardy's Wessex* (1913) – included in the definitive Wessex edition of Thomas Hardy's works.

Hermann Lea was remembered for his generosity and his unconventionality, for his compassion and his acute observation. He died at Linwood in the New Forest where he had lived for his last thirty years.

Hermann Lea

The Hardy Guides

A Guide to the West Country

Volume 1

Edited by Gregory Stevens Cox

Penguin Books

Penguin Books Ltd, Harmondsworth, Middlesex, England
Viking Penguin Inc., 40 West 23rd Street, New York, New York 10010, U.S.A.
Penguin Books Australia Ltd, Ringwood, Victoria, Australia
Penguin Books Canada Limited, 2801 John Street, Markham, Ontario, Canada L3R 1B4
Penguin Books (N.Z.) Ltd, 182-190 Wairau Road, Auckland 10, New Zealand

First published 1986

Conceived and produced by Pilot Productions Limited, 59 Charlotte Street, London

Editorial assistance by Paul Reiderman
Route maps drawn by Rob Shone
Design assistance by Safu Maria Gilbert

Made and printed in Great Britain by Purnell & Sons Limited, Bristol
Duotone reproduction by Anglia Reproductions, Witham, Essex
Typeset in Palatino and Univers by Dorchester Typesetting Limited, Dorchester, Dorset

CONTENTS

EDITOR'S INTRODUCTION

In the last third of the nineteenth century Thomas Hardy composed a sequence of novels, short stories and poems about human life and destiny in rural Wessex. Since his vision was a mixture of the poetic and historical he regularly took local stories about real people, reworking this factual basis into a fictional form.

This process can easily be demonstrated by examining the novel *Tess of the d'Urbervilles* where the action of the story is precipitated by the antiquarian researches of Parson Tringham of Stagfoot Lane, who discovered that John Durbyfield was a descendant of the d'Urberville family. In fact there actually lived a Reverend Bingham in Victorian Dorset. He was the incumbent of Bingham's Melcombe, a parish that incorporated the hamlet of Hartfoot Lane and the manor which anciently belonged to the Turbervils. The process of transformation could not be more apparent. The factual Reverend Bingham, Hartfoot Lane and the Turbervils become the fictional Parson Tringham, Stagfoot Lane and the d'Urbervilles respectively. This literary transmutation can be demonstrated throughout the Wessex works of Hardy. As the landscape and buildings of Hardy's Wessex were firmly based on the reality of the South West of England, it is not surprising that by the 1890's enthusiasts were already making literary pilgrimages to Wessex in search of the real lanes, roads, rivers, weirs, houses, farms, inns, prisons, graveyards, churches, barns, harbours, cliffs, hills and woods of fictional Wessex. Several guide books for literary pilgrims were published in the early twentieth century, of which by far the most important was *Thomas Hardy's Wessex* by Hermann Lea. Its importance lies in Lea's close friendship with Thomas Hardy and the novelist's active collaboration. Before discussing his *vade-mecum* to Wessex we should make a little excursion into the life and times of Lea.

Hermann Lea was born on the 12 February, 1869 at Thorpe-le-Soken in Essex. When a young man he became a pupil of Mr Wood Homer at Athelhampton Hall, Dorset, to learn farming and finding himself, by pure coincidence, living in the parish of Puddletown, the Weatherbury of

Far From the Madding Crowd. Later in his life Lea was to write that here "the utter realism of Hardy's writing forced itself" upon him.

Lea's first glimpse of the great author, which only prompted a few words of mutual apology, was when in August 1888 Lea almost collided with Hardy in a stationer's door in Dorchester.

There then passed ten years of "fitful vicissitude" during which Lea familiarised himself with the Wessex novels and the "topographical features therein displayed." He took up photography, joining the Dorset Photographic Club where he met the club secretary, the Reverend Thomas Perkins who was the rector of Turnworth. Perkins was also an enthusiast of the Wessex novels and soon the two admirers had hatched the idea of sets of picture postcards illustrating the stories. Perkins arranged a lunch party at which he introduced Lea to Hardy. The postcard plan was mentioned and Lea was later to record the sequel:

> Hardy was distinctly interested in our scheme, and we discussed together which of the novels should be chosen for the initial venture, and which of the scenes in the selected volumes should be portrayed.
>
> From that day Hardy took an active part in our venture, and many were the excursions we made together, mostly by cycle, sometimes on foot, to choose and photograph the actual subject. Here, of course, he was exceedingly helpful in identifying some of the less obvious spots, always insisting on our bearing carefully in mind the fact that they only represented the scenes from which he had, more or less exactly, sketched the backgrounds described in his books.
>
> In addition to these specific outings I had many opportunities for reaching a yet more intimate acquaintance with Hardy. We met at Max Gate, at the houses of mutual friends, by chance encounters.

This friendship was to last for the rest of Hardy's life, some thirty years, during which Lea and Hardy met close on a thousand times. The importance of the friendship is attested by independent sources. Sir Newman Flower wrote that whenever Thomas Hardy spoke to him about Hermann Lea "it was always in terms of warm friendship and regard for what he had done."

The friendship was based on a mutual interest in a wide range of matters concerning Dorset, its customs, superstitions, folklore and the dialect and its etymology. Hardy hated cruelty to animals and congratulated Lea on being a vegetarian. Above all they were united by a love for the Dorset landscape. Lea's autobiographical notes include

Hardy's Map of the Wanderings of Tess

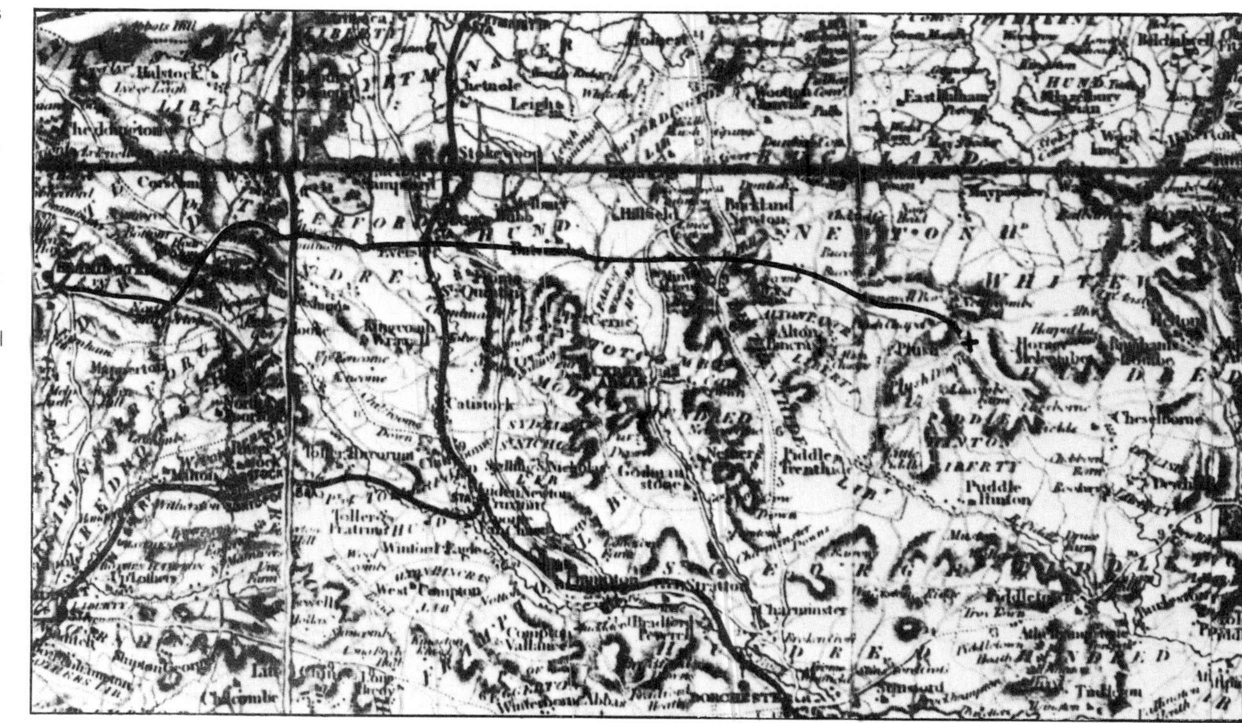

Using this photograph of Hardy's own map it is possible to offer a solution to the whereabouts of *Flintcomb-Ash*, the fictional place where Tess stayed before setting off to Beaminster in search of news about Clare (see Hardy's cross). However, the controversy (as much an issue in Lea's day as it is today, and a sign of just how closely it is possible to walk in the footsteps of so many of Hardy's fictional characters) cannot be solved wholly since Hardy's actual description in *Tess* does conform to Lea's contradictory conclusion on page 35 following. See Tess's route from *Flintcomb-Ash* to Beaminster.

the following entry under the heading 1900. It is quoted at length as it uniquely evokes the atmosphere of the Lea-Hardy excursions:

> On a glorious early autumn morning – 18 September, 1900 – Mr and Mrs Hardy and her niece, Miss Gifford, cycled over to Bardolf. We were bound for Bulbarrow. Mrs Hardy being a little tired, I drove her, together with our lunch, Mrs Wood Homer and the others cycling.
>
> Hardy mentioned that it used to be a matter of dispute whether Bulbarrow was the highest, or only the second-highest, point in Dorset. From it extends a wonderful panorama in all directions and we spent an interesting time picking out, with the aid of glasses, numerous features which had served him as models for description in the Wessex Novels. Villages, hills, valleys, tumuli – one after another we identified them, and Hardy explained to me why their particular features claimed his special attention, why they had attracted him, how the fictitious names had suggested themselves to his mind. It was many years since he had visited this spot, and this was the first time he had searched the landscape with the aid of glasses. The atmospheric conditions were particularly helpful, and he was surprised at the number of distant features that revealed themselves, becoming quite excited at each fresh discovery. He also made mention of a number of other high points which we must certainly visit later, bidding me not to forget to bring my glasses. These high view-points, I was to discover later, formed a particular attraction to him, and subsequent outings were frequently chosen by him with this end in view. In the course of the years that followed, we visited many high view-points in the district, including: High Stag, Rainbarrow, Hardy Monument . . .

Hardy must have found Lea an interesting character for the latter was something of a Victorian eccentric. Remembered by his nephew for his "generosity, independence of thought, strong compassion, unconventional habits, complete indifference to popular opinion, strong streak of Rabelaisian humour and great strength of will", Lea was a builder, beekeeper, gardener, poultry-keeper, ardent cyclist, water-diviner, animal lover, inventor, photographer, author and automobilist. His first car, a red Oldsmobile with a dangerous kick in its starting operation, was replaced in 1901 by a Hupmobile. Lea frequently acted as chauffeur to Hardy as they motored thousands of miles across Wessex.

In 1904 Lea was invited by a publisher to produce a series of maps suggesting road tours in Hardy's Wessex with the instructions that "short descriptive letterpress, and photographs of the places themselves, was to accompany the sketch-maps." Lea wrote to Hardy to secure permission for the venture and Thomas Hardy "although lukewarm at first . . . eventually became quite interested." This resulted in a volume entitled *A Handbook to the Wessex Country of Thomas Hardy's Novels and Poems* (1905).

Some five years later Messrs Macmillan were preparing a uniform and definitive edition of Hardy's works. It was decided to produce a companion volume on the topography of the Wessex novels and poems and Lea was commissioned to write this official study, a task which he took seriously. Again it is appropriate to quote from his autobiographical notes:

> Although I had visited most of these towns and villages and natural features, and had, moreover, a fairly wide selection of photographs covering the historical Wessex, there were still some places that demand identification. Thus between 1910 and 1913, when the book was first published, my task necessitated many and frequent visits to Max Gate. As the work proceeded, Hardy grew increasingly interested and I found him ever ready to help with suggestions, particularly in regard to which subjects should be used for illustration.
>
> Sometimes he wrote me notes regarding the places; sometimes he gave me information during my visits to Max Gate; and sometimes he came with me to look at certain somewhat obscure features to which he had referred in his writings, and which he himself was not too certain about.

The fruit of this labour was *Thomas Hardy's Wessex*, first published in 1913. Hardy himself had corrected the proofs of the book to ensure that there were no inaccuracies.

The artist is not bound by the actual. Hardy once told Lea that as a writer he had always striven to attempt description "only of such things as he had actually experienced or learned by actual first-hand knowledge." However, it must be remembered that Hardy sometimes transferred an identifiable building to another district and combined into one building the different architectural features of two buildings. This transposition sometimes makes exact identification impossible. In 1904 Hardy wrote to Lea "I have again and again denied that the fictitious places *are* such and such real ones, but are merely ideal places suggested by them" [Hardy letter now in Sanders collection, Dorset County Museum].

It is also important to recognise that occasionally Hardy and Lea resisted making too precise an identification for three principal reasons. First, already by the Edwardian period, hordes of Hardy pilgrims were making their way to the heart of Wessex. In order to protect relatives and friends from over-eager visitors Hardy and Lea declined to pinpoint certain houses and cottages especially in the

Stinsford area. Second, it must be remembered that Hardy drew on real stories involving people still alive, or only recently dead. On occasions, therefore, he would blur identification in order to frustrate literary detectives seeking to solve a *roman à clef*. Perhaps the most obvious example of this involves *The Woodlanders*, a novel set in the Melbury Bubb area of West Dorset. It was the village from which Hardy's mother had originally come and close to the ancestral home of Lord Ilchester. As Hardy was a friend of the Ilchester family and had no wish to upset any of its members, he accordingly made topographical corrections in succeeding editions of *The Woodlanders* and distanced Hintock House from the Melbury Bubb district. Finally, in the case of two or three of his localities, even Hardy was uncertain about the original place that he once had in mind when he came to identify the invented names for Lea. [The Hardy-Lea correspondence displays such an uncertainty over *A Group of Noble Dames*.]

Of Lea's identifications some ninety-nine per cent have always been accepted as canonical. Of the remaining one per cent it has sometimes been contended that Lea was in error. In my opionion this is a misunderstanding of the nature of Lea's *opus*. *Thomas Hardy's Wessex* is the identification as wished by Hardy himself. As regards the contested identifications we are dealing either with a fictional building whose features are drawn from two or more real buildings, or a protected location as stated above. Naturally it is possible to try to clarify Hardy's obfuscation, which entails a close comparison of Hardy's original manuscript with several serial versions and early book editions of the novels and short stories. The bibliography below gives details of some of these textual studies. It should be noted that Hardy did not originally conceive a complete and consistent topography for his fictional Wessex, letting it evolve as he created the works. Subsequently a certain amount of standardisation was imposed by him in the definitive *Wessex Edition* (Macmillan, 1912).

Thomas Hardy's Wessex is the product of a literary friendship and a singularly happy set of coincidences: Lea loved Hardy's works; he was an enthusiastic photographer and lived in Dorset; he had the time and opportunity to travel through Wessex from end to end, and he received the active help of Hardy himself. Though there are critics who disparage Hardy because his fictional plots sometimes revolve on coincidence, such critics are usually blind to the myriad coincidences, both malign and benign, which frequently attend human endeavours.

I have one concluding thought. We are living in a period

of rapid and violent change. Perhaps the best tribute that we can actively pay to Thomas Hardy today is to take *Thomas Hardy's Wessex* as one of our textbooks of what should be protected and conserved in the West of England. The landscape should not be further scarred. The buildings mentioned in Lea's book should be designated and scheduled as protected, if not already so listed, and while this may incur the wrath of the developers it will at least elicit the gratitude of our children.

G.S.C.

Thomas Hardy in pensive mood,
at Max Gate.

INTRODUCTION

The object of this book, as its title indicates, is to depict the Wessex country of Thomas Hardy, with a view to discovering the real places which served as bases for the descriptions of scenery and backgrounds given us in the novels and poems. But before commencing our survey I should like to direct attention to certain facts which it seems necessary to grasp for the proper understanding of such discoveries as we shall presently make.

To begin, we will take a general glance at the tract of country covered by our author. There has been an impression current amongst some people that Thomas Hardy's Wessex is limited to the county of Dorset, but we have it on his own assurance that the Wessex of the novels and poems is practically identical with the Wessex of history, and includes the counties of Berkshire, Wilts, Somerset, Hampshire, Dorset, and Devon – either wholly or in part. We are told in the preface to "A Pair of Blue Eyes" that "the shore and country about 'Castle Boterel' (approximately Boscastle) is the farthest westward of all those convenient corners wherein I have ventured to erect my theatre . . . and it lies near to, or no great way beyond, the vague border of the Wessex kingdom." The author's ingenious disinterment of the old name leads us to consider for a moment the actual boundaries of this former kingdom. They can only be guessed at. According to the Saxon Chronicle, the kingdom was founded by the Prince Cerdic and Cynric his son, who landed in the year 494, and who, after some successful battles against the Welsh, became kings in 519. We have only conjecture to go upon, but it seems probable that southern Hampshire and the Isle of Wight were the earliest locations. Whether Cerdic – a name probably of Welsh origin – actually founded the kingdom of Wessex must remain a matter for debate. But wherever it was founded, and by whomsoever, we have a certain amount of testimony to prove that its boundaries were considerably expanded during the reign of Ceawlin (560 to 592), and in 571 Aylesbury and the upper part of the Thames Valley were conquered by the West Saxons; and again, in 577, Cirencester, Bath, and Gloucester likewise succumbed. A large portion of Somerset was annexed by Cenwalh (643 to 672), and by the end of the seventh century the rest of that county and certain parts of Devonshire were added. The area now reached is that usually shown on maps, and roughly corresponds with that adopted by our author. During the reign of Ecgberht (808 to 836) Sussex, Surrey, Kent, and Essex became an integral portion of Wessex. Then followed an interval during which there were further annexations, certain divisions, some reunions, until in 871 the whole kingdom passed to Alfred, except such parts as were under Danish rule.

In 878 a peace was established between Alfred of Wessex and the Danes, by which it was agreed that the boundary line should be regarded as the Thames, northward up the Lea to its source, thence to Bedford, and along the Ouse to Watling Street – the old Roman road from London to Chester. By this treaty, London, Middlesex and part of Hertford, became an absolute part of Wessex. During the years of comparative peace which ensued, Alfred inaugurated the first attempts at defensive warfare, as well as a restoration of the schools. Later he was engaged in active warfare with the Danes, and when he died in 900 he left the kingdom of Wessex still unconquered. From that time, Edward the Elder, his son, worked hard in subduing the Danes and absorbing them among his own subjects until the year 918, when the last of the Danish Kings of East Anglia was slain, and that realm annexed. Then followed many vicissitudes ending in the Norman Conquest.

It is now more than twenty years since I first became interested in tracing the topographical features of the Wessex Novels, and as I have lived in Wessex continuously during that period, and have travelled over practically all the main roads, and many of the lanes and by-roads – traversing more than 150,000 miles on a cycle, in a car, on foot – I have had peculiar opportunities for following out my hobby. In 1904 I wrote a small guide-book to such portions of the scenery as came within the boundary of Dorset; but this was in no sense exhaustive, and dealt only with some of the principal backgrounds. For the purposes of the present book I have revisited every one of the spots described.

My attention has frequently been drawn to inexactitudes or misstatements that have appeared in the many guide-books to the Wessex country which have already been published. These have very likely arisen through a desire on the part of the writer to make the fictitious places conform to the real in an absolute, dogmatic manner. Should any such inaccuracies have crept into the present book I must ask my readers' kindly indulgence. I have not

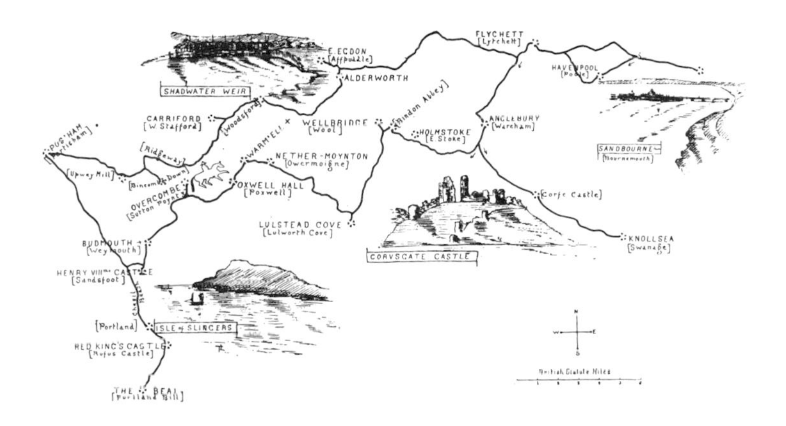

The Southern Tract – the First Route through Wessex Suggested by Lea

read any of the published guide-books, fearing lest I might be led into a form of plagiarism which would be distasteful. References have been made to certain county histories and other recognised works of authority, but the bulk of the descriptions have been written on the actual spots visited.

To those who desire to follow an itinerary with detailed exactitude I would suggest reference to the one-inch ordnance maps of the district. These furnish all neccessary information as to roads, lanes, paths, woodlands, and hills.

In the text of the Wessex Novels are many dialectic words, phrases, and idioms, most of which may still be heard occasionally in the remoter districts. Probably, as William Barnes held, the speech of Dorset and the adjoining counties was the outcome of the Anglo-Saxon language rather than a mere dialect, nearly all of the words being traceable to their origin. The New Oxford Dictionary includes a number of these dialectic expressions which have been supplied by the author of the Wessex volumes.

The task of writing this book has been a very pleasant one, providing many interesting experiences; and my thanks are due to those who have aided me, either by giving information or by permitting me to photograph their houses. To more than any one else I am indebted to Mr. Hardy himself for correcting me in a few identifications of some of the places which, owing to the meagre clues in the text, defied discovery by any other means.

In regard to the more intimate details which we are setting out to elucidate, it may be said first that with the

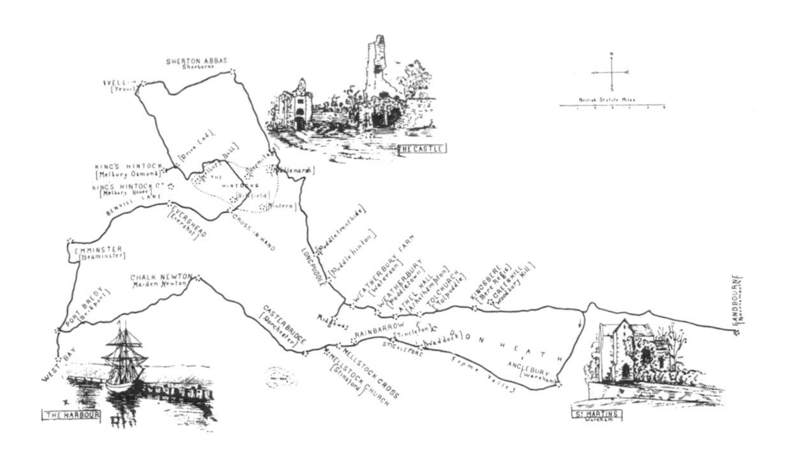

The Midmost Tract – the Second Route through Wessex Suggested by Lea

characters themselves I have, of course, nothing to do. This may appear an unnecessary observation, till I mention that more than one curious inquirer has asked me whether such-or-such a character in one of the stories is not intended to be a portrait of X—, and has than given the name of a person living in or near the place which the fictitious name is supposed to represent. Next, the houses, churches, and other architectural features which are to claim our attention are plainly not each depicted from one real model – for some are undoubtedly composite structures. In some cases there are distinct clues from which we may draw our deductions: described peculiarities in the fabric of a building; the interchange of place and character names; the construction of the name itself, relating to some obvious characteristic of a town or village. The natural configurations, such as the hills, heaths, downs, and woods, are, for the most part, so faithfully pictured that we may venture to be almost dogmatic in reconciling them with their counterparts, while many of them appear under their established names.

Nevertheless, I want to make it very clear at the outset that the descriptions given in the novels and poems must be regarded in their totality as those of imaginative places. The exact Wessex of the books exists nowhere outside them, as Mr. Hardy himself indeed has hinted. Thus, instead of declaring *Casterbridge* to *be* Dorchester, we dare only say that the presentment is undoubtedly founded on salient traits in the real town. Certain stages, certain scenery and backgrounds, are essential to the setting of every drama, but it has been left for Thomas Hardy to

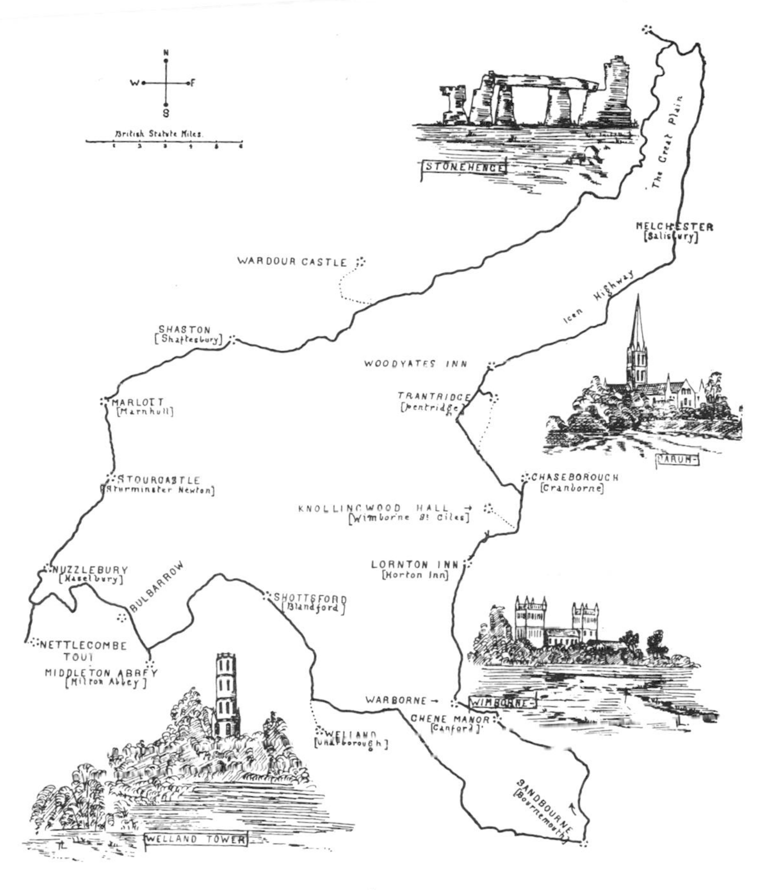

The Northern Tract – the Third Route through Wessex Suggested by Hermann Lea

describe such accessories in a manner that probably no other writer, before or since, has ever accomplished. This fact it is which makes our work both easier and at the same time more interesting. The realistic treatment which the setting of the stories receives creates rather a dangerous position for the topographer, since there is an undoubted tendency to fall into the error of confusing the ideal with the actual.

Should any disappointment arise in the minds of those who visit the existing places – on account of any want of similarity between these and the book descriptions – he may be reminded, in addition, that most of the stories were written many years ago, and that, in the interval which has now elapsed, Time and the hand of man have been responsible for many alterations, and have brought about actual obliterations of what were close originals at the date of portrayal. When the Wessex writer first turned his attention to verse and fiction he can have had no conception of the prominence to which he would attain among living authors – nor could he have anticipated the searching nature of the investigations that would be made into the scenery which served him as pattern.

There is another point to which I should like to draw attention, and that is the strange manner in which the scenery adapts itself to, and identifies itself with, the characters themselves. We have a striking instance of this in the life-history of Tess. Her child-character develops at *Marlott* (Marnhull), an unsophisticated village somewhat isolated from the outside world, remote from any large town, and where she is little prepared to cope with a man of the world such as Alec d'Urberville. It is in the sombre shades of Cranborne Chase, dark with its primeval yews and oaks, that her betrayal is effected. It is in the Froom Valley, within sight and sound of the crystal streams, where the grass grows lush and the air is fragrant with the scents of many flowers – the whole scene typical of growth – that we find the creation and expansion and maturing of that all-absorbing love which was to remain with her throughout her life. It is at *Wellbridge* that her repulse by Clare and her realisation of the full bitterness of life comes to her – that ancient home of her ancestors, a place filled with associations of a mouldy past, the home of those gruesome portraits, where the very atmosphere seems to be charged with things sinister. The phase of her hopelessness finds her at *Flintcomb-Ash*, a spot cursed by sterility, where Nature looks with an unkindly eye, and blesses not the labour of man's hand. When in utter despair she becomes callous and joins d'Urberville, it is at *Sandborne* we find her – that place of "fashionable promenades and new villas." And at last, when the officers of the law demand her as a victim to the merciless Mosaic recrimination dictated by a lust for revenge, the scene is Stonehenge, where the ancient Druids, the representatives of a god whose anger and love of destruction could only be appeased by the shedding of innocent blood, had sacrificed their thousands. We have only touched on a few instances, but the other scenes are equally appropriate.

H. L.

THE COUNTRY OF

"TESS OF THE D'URBERVILLES"

This being the most widely read of the Wessex Novels, it is convenient to place it first in the examination of their scenery and backgrounds. The action takes place over a wide stretch of country – from Salisbury Plain in the north to Dorchester in the south; from the New Forest in the east to Beaminster in the west. In leading my readers over the ground covered by the different scenes, and in pointing out certain towns, villages, houses, and natural landmarks, it must be clearly understood – as I have already shown in the Introduction – that these are merely originals which approximate to the imaginative backgrounds set up by our author. In the volume with which we are now dealing such features have been rendered more realistically than in some others, and accordingly we find little difficulty in reconciling the actual with the ideal.

The story opens by introducing us to John Durbeyfield as he journeys homewards to *Marlott* from *Shaston*, and the meeting with Parson Tringham, "the antiquary of Stagfoot Lane (Hartfoot Lane)," which reveals to him that the name of Durbeyfield is synonymous with d'Urberville – obviously a close imitation of the real name of a family now extinct in the county.

We will precede Durbeyfield and enter the village of *Marlott* (Marnhull, more or less). It "lay amid the north-eastern undulations of the beautiful Vale of Blakemoor or Blackmoor . . . in which the fields are never brown and the springs never dry." The "Forest of the White Hart" is an alternative name for the valley which our author occasionally employs. Marnhull would seem to be a corruption of its original name of Marlhill, a more significant title, referring apparently to the white clay or marl which crops up there and which, after exposure to the air, hardens into a freestone. The church and many of the houses are built of it. Marnhull was once quite a considerable place; the remains of many streets may be traced where the houses have entirely disappeared. The dwellings now are curiously disconnected, many wide gaps intervening, but new buildings are rapidly springing up, and the village bids fair to assume its old size at no very distant date. Its old notoriety for drunkenness and general debauchery has now passed away, and it is no longer known as "the booziest place in Dorset."

The Crown, Marnhull *(The Pure Drop Inn, Marlott)*
"There's a very pretty brew in tap at the Pure Drop." Little altered since the end of the last century, its "pure drop bar" leaves the visitor in little doubt that it was the model used by Hardy.

The Blackmoor Vale Inn, Marnhull *(Rollivers)*
The inspiration for Rollivers stands about one mile north west of the church but has been completely rebuilt since Hardy's day.

Marnhull *(Marlott)*
Does Lea claim that the cottage "appears to have been swept away" simply to assuage Hardy's genuine concern that its real inhabitants should not be disturbed by tourists? There are those who do not doubt the truth of a story in which the elderly Hardy, while standing outside Barton Cottage (known as Tess's cottage today) replied to an inquisitive gardener that he was "only seeing where I put my Tess".

Here we meet Tess for the first time, "in her right hand a peeled willow wand, and in her left a bunch of white flowers," making her way with the other village maidens to the field where the Maydance was to take place. Towards them came Durbeyfield, driving in a vehicle belonging to the *Pure Drop* Inn. This inn figures many times in the book, and may, by its position in the village, be recognised as "The Crown." *Rolliver's*, the other inn mentioned, would seem to be suggestive of the "Blackmoor Vale Inn," on the western and lower side of the straggling village.

The only other feature with which we have to deal at the moment is the old cottage in which Tess was imagined to have been born, but this, alas, appears to have been swept away. From the description of its situation we may assume that it stood at the end of the village nearest to Shaftesbury. At this village, too, Angel Clare comes on the stage; and we are made acquainted with Mrs. Durbeyfield and the younger children.

The next background in Tess's history with which we are concerned is exhibited when she starts for *Casterbridge* (Dorchester) very early in the morning to deliver the load of bee-hives. After passing the little town of *Stourcastle* (approximately Sturminster Newton) the road rises steadily towards Hazelbury Bryan – a village we shall visit later. *Stourcastle* is never more to us than a halting-place, though there is some historical interest attaching to it.

A hamlet near by was the birthplace of William Barnes, the Dorset poet, a statue of whom stands in the church close of St. Peter's at Dorchester. Sturminster Newton was the home of Robert Young, "An olde Dorset Songster," whose poems, written under the pseudonym of "Rabin Hill," have lately been collected and published in a small volume. Just outside the town, on the other side of the river Stour, is a mound, the site of a castle where King Alfred is said to have lived. Near by is a picturesque old mill, one of the few of its kind remaining in Wessex.

A few miles beyond *Stourcastle* Tess and Abraham came in sight of Bulbarrow, rising high on their left hand. This camp has a circular, double entrenchment, generally supposed to be of Celtic origin. It is the second highest point in Dorset. From its summit extends on all sides a magnificent view, the eyes of the beholder penetrating far over Dorset into the adjoining counties. Many places interesting to Hardy readers can be identified from here with the aid of a glass, and amongst others is "the hill-town called Shaston."

It is to this place that Tess walks when she goes to visit her reputed relative; and from here she rides in the

The Mill, Sturminster Newton
(Stourcastle)
The poems by Rabin Hill, to which Lea alludes, were composed by Robert Young (1811-1908). "Rabin Hill" was a poetical pseudonym. A collection of his poems was edited by the Rev. J. C. M. Mansell-Pleydell and published in Dorchester in 1910. The mill at Sturminster Newton (*Stourcastle*) is still in use – though no longer powered by water.

Pentridge Church *(Trantridge)*
Pentridge (the *Trantridge* where "the mysterious Mrs d'Urberville had her residence") lies at the end of a by-road running south-east from the main Salisbury-Blandford road. Since Hardy's day, the village has become a cul-de-sac of almost impenetrable solitude.

carrier's van which travelled to *Chaseborough* and passed near *Trantridge* (suggesting Pentridge) – "the parish in which the vague and mysterious Mrs. d'Urberville had her residence." *Shaston* enters largely into the book entitled "Jude the Obscure," and our only present interest in it is when, on her return journey, Tess slept the night "at the house of a cottage woman they knew." The actual cottage is not further indicated and we must leave its position unidentified. If we approach the town towards evening from the direction of Cranborne we shall see it just as our author describes it, "standing majestically on its height; its windows shining like lamps in the evening sun."

The house to which Tess was journeying, known in the story as *The Slopes*, was situated near the little village of *Trantridge* on the borders of Cranborne Chase. We may regard this house as purely imaginary, or at least as having been drawn from a model in some other district, for there is no house here answering to the description, though there is one near Wimborne. This village also figures in one of "Life's Little Ironies." It lies about three miles from Cranborne and is close to the Wiltshire boundary. Its name is derived from the British word Pen, meaning a head or the principal part, and hence the apex of a hill; close to it is Penbury Hill, where a beacon once stood.

The next place presented is when Tess goes with the other work-people to spend a Saturday evening at *Chaseborough* (nearly Cranborne), and stands late at night waiting for them to start homewards. Cranborne is the market town of the district; it was famous both in Saxon and Norman times for its monastery; the church now in existence is one of the oldest and largest in the county of Dorset. It is partly Norman, partly Early English, with some later Perpendicular work, and contains many interesting tablets and monuments. The curfew is rung every night except on Sunday, and following it the date of the month is tolled. The fine Tudor manor-house which stands near the church takes the place of a building which was one of the favourite resorts of King John; some of the internal walls may possibly be of that king's date. The name Cranborne is supposedly derived from Anglo-Saxon words denoting "crane" and "river" – the winding of the river here suggesting somewhat the neck of a crane. Previous to the construction of the Western Turnpike the high road from London to the west led directly through the town. It is still an excellent road, and is praised as such in "Barbara," in "A Group of Noble Dames," of which anon. The only feature of the town which particularly interests the Hardy student is the *Flower-de-Luce* Inn, where Alec d'Urberville discovered Tess waiting for her

Fleur-de-Lys, Cranborne *(The Flower-de-Luce, Chaseborough)*
The *Flower-de-Luce*, as it was called in *Tess* (Fleur-de-Lis, in Hardy's day) is hardly altered since Alec d'Urbeville found Tess waiting there for her friends.

Typical Text of "the Text-Writer"
Today's text – should any be found – is unlikely to carry so Calvinist a theme.

companions. Its prototype, the "Fleur-de-Lis," is readily discovered, the name being often now, and formerly always, pronounced as spelt in the novel.

We are now brought to the environment of the first real tragedy in Tess's career – when she found herself at the mercy of Alec d'Urberville. *The Chase* (Cranborne Chase) was a chase proper, and must not be confused with a forest – a prerogative of kingly right. It embraces an area of some 800,000 acres and is "the oldest wood in England." One may readily wander for mile after mile in this ancient Chase without meeting a single human being; and although certain tracts have been brought under cultivation, there is a tendency for these to revert again to forest. No fitter scene could have been chosen for such an episode.

Subsequently we follow Tess back to *Marlott*, when she meets the text-writer – an individual who is by no means extinct at the present day. On many a gate and stile in the Wessex lanes and by-ways we may discover evidences of his industry in quotations more or less apt, but nearly all of gloomy, Calvinistic significance. Once again in her old home, we find her sensitive nature seeking refuge in the bedroom which she shared with some of the other children. We see the fields wherein she worked by day, and the hill-sides and the woods to which she wandered by night. It is here, at *Marlott*, that her baby is born, and here that it dies and is buried "in that shabby corner of God's allotment where He lets the nettles grow." There is no stone to mark the place of burial and as the churchyard to-day is scrupulously neat and well cared for, its appearance at the date of the story can only be imagined. Down to the third quarter of the last century, however, such corners were often reserved in country churchyards for that reprobate class of person designated.

Our next scene is at the dairy at *Talbothays*, the location of which has evoked considerable controversy amongst those who have attempted to identify the places mentioned in the Wessex Novels. It may be stated definitely that the dairy-house is drawn from no particular building, but that it is typical of many of the dairies which occur in the Froom Valley. We are informed that it lay in "The Valley of the Great Dairies, the valley in which milk and butter grew to rankness . . . the verdant plain so well watered by the river Var or Froom" From the summit of a hill only a short distance from *Weatherbury* (largely Puddletown as it formerly was) Tess first saw her future place of sojourn. The picture before her was a complete contrast to the one she had gazed upon from childhood: there everything was of smaller proportions – smaller

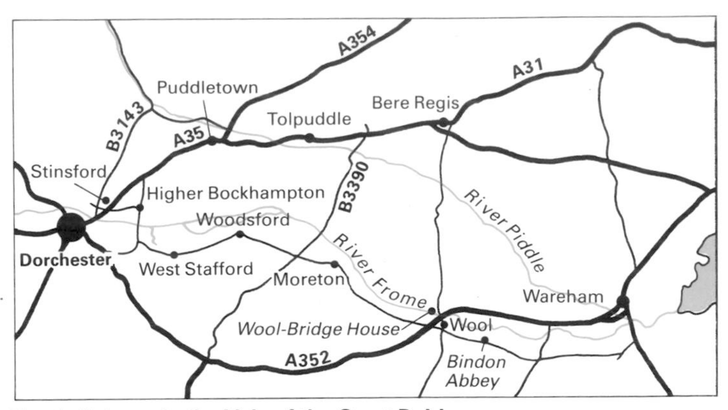

Tess's Sojourn in the Vale of the Great Dairies

The Frome Valley *(The Valley of the Great Dairies)*
"The world was drawn to a larger pattern here. The enclosures numbered fifty acres instead of ten, the farmsteads were more extended, the groups of cattle formed tribes hereabout; there (Blackmoor Vale) only families . . . It lacked the intensely blue atmosphere of the rival vale and its heavy soils and scents; the new air was clear, bracing, ethereal."

The Dairy at *Talbothays*
Lea maintains that Talbothays farm was drawn "from no particular building". However, another of Hardy's friends, Clive Holland, claimed that Hardy had in mind Norris Mill Farm. The mystery is further complicated by the claim of a recent researcher, Denys Kay-Robinson, that Lower Lewell Farm was its true model.

fields, smaller herds of cows; here were vast stretches of water-meads, huge herds of cows. The peculiar difference in the atmosphere is also strikingly noticeable: the Valley of the Froom, watered by the swiftly flowing river, is lighter, clearer, altogether more brilliant in appearance than the Blackmoor Vale, which always seems to strike the traveller afresh with a certain sense of oppressive heaviness, the stiffer nature of the soil adding to the feeling.

The description in the novel of the position occupied by the dairy in relation to other landmarks would seem to indicate that, in the writer's fancy, the spot lay at no great distance from the junction of the Dorchester-Tincleton and Puddletown-Ilsington roads, on the southern margin of *Egdon Heath*, and in full view of Rainbarrows – a section of country which will have our further attention when we treat of "The Dynasts" and "The Return of the Native." This location of *Talbothays* is sufficiently indicative to enable us to follow Tess in thought as she goes about her various duties at the dairy, or when, in her hours of leisure, she wanders with Angel Clare "along the meads by creeping paths which followed the brinks of trickling tributary brooks." It may be mentioned that "Talbots" or "Talbothays" ("hays" means hedges) is the real name of a small freehold estate in the neighbourhood that was owned by our author's father at the time the story was written, and is still in the possession of a member of his family; but at that date there was no house standing upon it, nor was ever a dairy there, then or since; so that the name only was borrowed.

The Froom Valley sweeps through Dorset from above Maiden Newton, till the river empties itself into the tidal estuary at Wareham, and contains the most fertile and valuable land of its kind in the country; the carefully tended irrigated meadows producing an abnormal amount of grass forage and supporting huge herds of cows. Many months, full-charged with happenings, passed over Tess during her stay in the Froom Valley – "that green trough of sappiness and humidity," and here we see the intimacy between her and Angel Clare passing from mere acquaintance to friendship, and from friendship to marriage. The latter's position in regard to the other dairymaids and the subsequent effect on their natures is also brought out here. The episode of Clare carrying the four girls through the water instances this point. They were on their way to the service at *Mellstock* (Stinsford) church, and he over-took them just as they reached that part of the road which was flooded with water. A portion of the road near Bockhampton Bridge lies very low and is often flooded in winter, so that we may be within reason

West Stafford Church
In a postcard note to Lea on 29 May, 1905, Hardy urged Lea to write "apparently" or "probably" if Woodsford church was proposed as the wedding place of Tess and Angel Clare. However, by the time of publication this seems to have been checked, as Lea does not waver in his opinion.

Wool-Bridge House
(Wellbridge House)
The house remains unchanged since the time when Tess and Angel entered it. "Of all the scenes . . . no place is so near to reality," said Lea.

in surmising that it was here the occurrence is supposed to have taken place.

West Stafford Church would seem to represent the place at which Tess and Clare were married. It is in its reality a building containing some interesting Jacobean woodwork. They had decided to spend the early days of their union at one of the ancestral homes of the d'Urbervilles. The way there is now, as then, along a level road that follows the river more or less closely until it nears the village of Wool. Then, turning to the left and passing "over the great Elizabethan bridge," we come upon *Wellbridge House* (Wool-Bridge House), clearly seen from the train as it enters the station of Wool. It is probable that, of all the scenes which occur throughout the Wessex Novels, no place is so near to reality or so familiar to my readers as this house. Inside it may be found the old mural portraits which had such an effect on Tess's imagination. Up to the time at which the novel was published they were quite distinct, but since then injudicious washing with soap to make them clearer has resulted in their being nearly obliterated altogether, though we can still trace the gruesomeness attributed to them. Interest of a psychical nature intrudes here, for I have it on the best of evidence that this weird effect actually does make itself felt on certain temperaments, people having told me of the ghastly dreams that have come to them after viewing these portraits. Another similar peculiarity attached to Wool-Bridge House is the legend of the coach. Clare had spoken of it, but had refrained from telling the whole story, and it is not until near the end of her life that Tess hears it fully, from the lips of Alec d'Urberville. According to local superstitions, it is said that the d'Urberville coach passes over the bridge hard by and draws up at the old house on Christmas Eve, but that the sound of its transit is only audible to the ears of certain individuals; also that it presages death or some dire calamity. I have known more than one local character declare that the house was haunted; though an old lady who lived there for some time practically alone told me she had never heard nor seen anything that could be regarded as preternatural. This evidence, however, counts for very little, only certain natures seeming to be gifted with the power of sensing psychic phenomena.

Soon after their entrance into the old house came to them the news of Retty Priddle's attempted suicide in the *Great Pool.* This we may well suppose to have been the same pool of which we have mention in "The Return of the Native," where it receives the name of *Shadwater Weir.*

Now comes before us the gloomy scenery of the second

Bindon Mill
"The Mill still worked on. The Abbey had perished." Writing to Lea on 26 April, 1905, Hardy commends Lea's choice of quotations which the latter had selected to accompany his photographs published as a set of postcards. In particular Hardy enjoyed the above quote accompanying this photograph of Bindon Mill, the place where Angel Clare worked to gain experience of the business.

Tess's Route to the Home of her Childhood

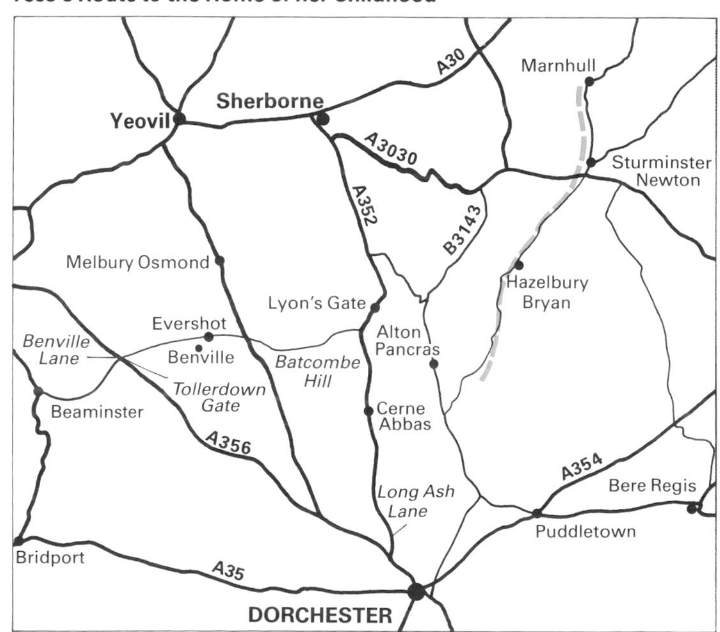

Meanwhile, Clare is pursuing his way westwards towards *Emminster* (Beaminster). This is our first visit to the place clearly indicated as "the hill-surrounded little town" with "the Tudor church-tower of red stone". Beaminster has been devastated by quite a number of conflagrations, but the Early English and Perpendicular church with its sculptured tower has always escaped undamaged. William Barnes gives us the following description of the town:

> Sweet Be'mi'ster, that bist a-bound
> By green an' woody hills all round,
> Wi' hedges, reachen up between
> A thousan' vields o' zummer green,
> Where elems' lofty heads do drow
> Their sheädes vor haÿ-meakers below,
> An' wild hedge-flow'rs do charm the souls
> O' maidens in their evenen strolls.

There is a curious custom still in vogue at Beaminster: on Sundays it is usual for many of the inhabitants to lock their doors when going to church and to leave the keys in the locks outside! The origin of this proceeding is obscure, but it may have arisen from the fact that some of the keys were ponderously heavy. Clare did not stay here long, but soon left the country for Brazil.

The next place to notice is a dairy near *Port-Bredy* (approximately Bridport). Of the exact location we have no knowledge, but we read it was situated "equally remote from her native place and from Talbothays." This is where Tess lives after her new departure from *Marlott*, but when work becomes difficult to obtain she decides to join Marian on "an upland farm in the centre of the county," and presently we see her starting to walk thither. "She reached *Chalk-Newton* (adumbrating Maiden Newton), and breakfasted at an inn." We shall visit Maiden Newton later (in Volume 2) when we are examining the country suggested by the descriptions in the short story entitled "Interlopers at the Knap," and it will suffice now to notice that little old hostel called the Castle Inn, standing close beside the river. Then Tess trudged on, until she drew near to Marian's place of sojourn – *Flintcomb-Ash*.

The actual position of *Flintcomb-Ash* has always been a debatable point with explorers in the Hardy country. To begin with, the farm-house cannot be pointed out, though such farm-houses do exist in the vicinity. But the actual site which served our author for his description is discoverable. If we will ascend the steep hill-side by a track leading out of Alton Pancras village to the eastward we shall soon reach a flat plateau. It is known locally as

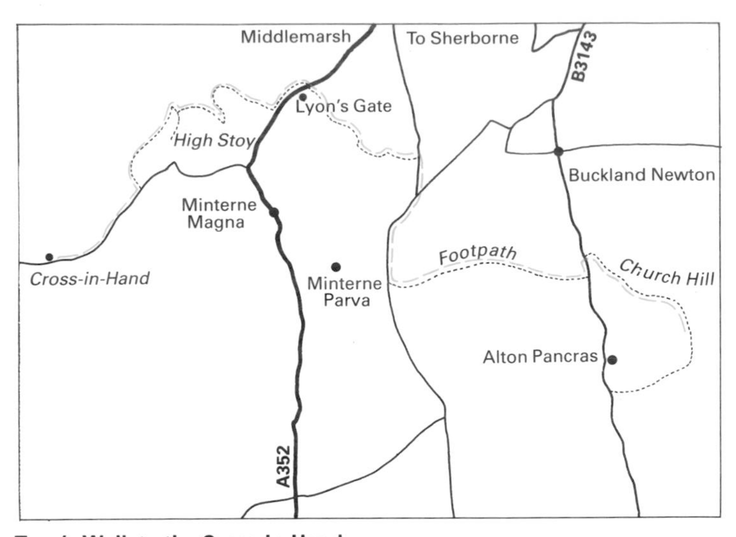

Tess's Walk to the Cross-in-Hand

The Cross-in-hand
"A strange rude monolith". Look out for this stone pillar whereon Tess placed her hand and swore never to tempt Alex d'Urberville before he "plunged into the valley in the direction of Abbot's-Cernel" (Cerne Abbas – see below). See "The Lost Pyx" for superstitions told to Lea by an old gypsy woman.

Barcombe Down. If we now follow along the crest of the hill we shall in due course light upon the ridged turf which marks the site of what was once a British village. For what reason the ancient people of Britain should have selected so bleak and unproductive a spot as this it is hard to determine. Marian described it as a "starve-acre" place – a title which is truthfully descriptive to-day. Vast numbers of flints lie uncovered on the chalky surface, making walking no easy matter, while the wind which sweeps over the plain greets the traveller with an unsympathetic touch. There is a sardonic aspect in the landscape, and the scene which stretches before us is all in harmony with the sufferings that Tess endured there.

It was after she had been at *Flintcomb-Ash* some little while that she determined to call at *Emminster* parsonage for tidings of Clare. The road she took was a rugged one, but quite practicable; a glance at the ordnance map will enable us to trace it exactly. From near the British Village a track-way descends by Church Hill to the high road; here we shall see a serpentine lane – Barn Lane – ascending the steep hill due westward. At its junction with the Sherborne-Dorchester road we must turn northwards for a little way, when we shall find another lane leading to the left. If we follow its windings, and cross the Sherborne-Cerne road at the point called Lyon's Gate, still making westward, we shall pass over High-Stoy and come in due course to the stone pillar Cross-in-Hand, or Crossy Hand as it is called locally. This is a walk which many people have taken since the publication of the story, and it will reward the pedestrian with a beautiful and varied prospect, the woodland that lies below to the northward including practically the whole of the background which serves for the novel entitled "The Woodlanders" – the country of *The Hintocks*. The diversity of landscape from right hand to left hand is truly amazing; the utter loneliness, the almost oppressive silence of Nature, add a weird touch which is intensified by coming suddenly upon this solitary landmark, Cross-in-Hand, springing up from the grassy down like the stem of a giant mushroom.

This stone pillar forms the *motif* of the poem entitled "The Lost Pyx," and I shall have occasion to refer to it further. Just now it stands before us as being the stone whereon Tess placed her hand when at Alec d'Urberville's demand, she swore never to tempt him. The occurrence, it will be remembered, took place on her return walk, d'Urberville coming thus far with her, and, after the oath had been registered, leaving her side to plunge into the valley in the direction of *Abbot's-Cernel* (Cerne Abbas). "Of all spots on the bleak and desolate upland this was the

The Cottage by the Church, Evershot *(Evershead)*
The cottage where Tess breakfasted on her way to *Emminster* (Beaminster) for tidings of Clare. See route-map illustration.

Blackmoor Vale *(The Vale of Little Dairies)*
"This fertile and sheltered tract of country, in which the fields are never brown and the springs never dry . . . Here, in the valley, the world seems to be constructed upon a smaller and more delicate scale; the fields are mere paddocks . . . the prospect is a broad rich mass of grass and trees . . ."

The Barn where Tess Heard Alec Preach
Today, all but the lower parts of its west and south walls have been demolished.

most forlorn," says our author – an estimate which I can endorse from personal observation; and I can also corroborate his finding "something sinister, or solemn, according to mood, in the scene amid which it stands."

Continuing her journey towards Clare's home, she would come in the course of three miles to another high road, called Long Ash Lane; crossing this, she would soon reach the village of *Evershead* (apparently Evershot). The "cottage by the church" at which she halted and breakfasted is obvious enough to the passer-by to-day. Benvill Lane, the real name of the second half of her route, leads up to "the edge of the basin in which Emminster and its Vicarage lay," where her resolution died and she fruitlessly retraced her steps.

The barn in which Alec d'Urberville, now "a excellent firey Christian man," was preaching was most probably drawn from the barn which stands near the centre of the village of Evershot and was originally used as a chapel. Tess heard him preaching as she passed through the village on her return walk. Still is also to be seen, beyond the northern part of Long Ash Lane, "the road ascending whitely to the upland along which the remainder of her journey lay."

A fresh landscape is led up to by Tess's route to the home of her childhood, where she goes on learning of the illness of her parents. A walk to Marnhull in the darkness from the place we have considered to be *Flintcomb-Ash* is no easy matter: fifteen miles of ascent and descent till Bulbarrow is mounted, and then a plunge down into the heavy-scented Blackmoor Vale. At *Nuttlebury* (Hazelbury Bryan) the village inn – bearing the sign of "The Antelope," we may remark – is passed as she passed it, and we trace "the maze of lanes she threaded" and re-enter Marnhull.

After the disasters that succeed one another here we follow her with all the family on a migration to *Kingsbere*. The loading of the waggon with their household goods and their journey along the road describes a scene which can be witnessed in Dorset any year on the 6th of April (Lady Day, old style), when the work-people move from farm to farm; the miscellaneous collection of goods useful and goods ornamental, with babies of various ages wedged in between pieces of furniture, as though to keep the latter from shifting about, is quite a common sight, and the emigrants often form veritable processions along the roads and lanes. Turning "the flank of an eminence which formed part of the upland called Greenhill" – scene of the fair in "Far from the Madding Crowd" – we dog them to the "half-dead townlet" – as our author designates

The Turberville Window, Bere Regis Church *(Kingsbere)*
"I've – got – gr't – family – vault – at – Kingsbere – and – Knighted – forefathers – in – lead – coffins – there" (John Durbeyfield).

Beaminster Vicarage
(Emminster Parsonage)
Both church (with its "Tudor Church-tower of red stone") and the vicarage shown here accord well today with the picture drawn by Hardy in Tess. Beaminster and its neighbourhood have been much loved by poets such as William Barnes and the late Edmund Blunden.

Bere Regis – where their ancestors reposed in the vaults beneath the church.

Kingsbere (Bere Regis), as its name indicates, was once a royal residence, and is supposed to have contained a palace belonging to Queen Elfrida; it was likewise a Roman station. The church is a fine building of flint and stone, chiefly Perpendicular in style, but with some Norman work in the interior; it was fairly well restored by G. E. Street many years ago. It contains three canopied tombs in Purbeck marble, as also a traceried window with heraldic emblems pertaining to the Turberville family. This obviously suggested the window of the novel under which the bedstead was erected. In the parish register may be seen the original signature of "Tho. Turberville," dated "May ye 10th 1679." The vaults of this family lie under the adjacent aisle, with an inscription in the entrance-stone, as mentioned in the book. They are now sealed up, but till lately people were living who had descended into them and had seen the coffins of generations of the name.

Clare's return to England, his short sojourn at *Emminster* Vicarage, and his search for Tess in the last phase of her life-history, gives us another lead through the landscapes. We may follow him as he leaves his father's house and proceeds along Benvill Lane, passes the *King's Hintock* (Melbury Osmund) estates, and the solitary pillar Cross-in-Hand, till he reaches *Flintcomb-Ash*, and thence goes to *Marlott* – localities we have already examined. We track him to *Shaston*, and to the little village in which he was informed the Durbeyfield family had settled, where he learns that Tess is at *Sandbourne* (Bournemouth). We duly follow him thither.

The description of this watering-place, with "its piers, its groves of pines, its promenades, and its covered gardens . . . like a fairy place suddenly created by the stroke of a wand, and allowed to get a little dusty," is well known, and is almost literal. The lodging-house called "The Herons," where Clare finds Tess, and where the great tragedy of the book is assumed to occur, it is impossible and undesirable to distinguish.

It is difficult to trace their flight – there being, of course, no tangible track of a pair "avoiding high-roads, and following obscure paths tending more or less northward . . . into the depths of the New Forest." They are said to have reached the empty house known as *Bramhurst Manor-house*. There are many such houses in the environs of Ringwood, but a careful examination persuades me that the mansion bears a strong resemblance, both in construction, furniture, and surroundings, to Moyle's Court – once the residence of Dame Alice Lisle, from which she was

Stonehenge
"The heathen temple . . . older than the centuries; older than the d'Urbervilles". Tess was finally arrested here and led away.

Winchester Gaol *(Wintoncester)*
"A large red-brick building, with level gray roofs, and rows of short barred windows . . . from the middle of the building an ugly flat-topped octagonal tower ascended." The milestone from where Angel and Liza-Lu waited "in paralysed suspense" for the final signal, is still there today, though the view of the gaol where Tess was executed is now obscured.

Moyle's Court, North of Ringwood *(Bramhurst Manor-House)*
In full flight, Tess and Angel arrive at Bramhurst Manor-house which as Moyle's Court is today a school, and rumoured still to be haunted by the spirit of Dame Alice Lisle. Both female residents – the fictional Tess and the historical Dame Alice – met an untimely end at Winchester (*Wintoncester*).

taken by the myrmidons of Jeffreys to her execution at Winchester. The house, by the way, is said to be still haunted by her spirit.

Their course northwards from here merges into clearness as they approach "the steepled city of *Melchester*" (approximately Salisbury). *Melchester* bulks more largely in "Jude the Obscure" and other of the Wessex Novels than in the present one, so that we need not pause to contemplate it now. "The graceful pile of cathedral architecture rose dimly on their left hand;"[1] they passed quickly through the city, and were soon following the road which led them to Salisbury Plain. They were now close to Stonehenge, the mysterious pagan temple, the greatest sight of its kind in the country. In the chronicles of Nennius (ninth century), the date of its origin is placed in the fifth century A.D.; but according to other and later writers it is supposed to have been erected one hundred years before Christ. Readers will not need to be reminded that there has been much controversy regarding its date and origin; no authentic proofs are forthcoming to establish any of the various contentions.

Here they are imagined to have waited till the morning dawned and Tess's pursuers came upon them and led her away towards *Wintoncester* (Winchester). This favoured city, which preserves much of its old-time historic interest, and over which the hand of the vandal has passed lightly, forms the last background we have to inspect. If we climb upon one of the hills close to the town we can verify the description given by our author. It still lies "amidst its convex and concave downlands"; there before us is the "sloping High Street," the "West Gateway," the "mediaeval cross," and "the bridge." We can go to-day to the top of the West Hill and find the milestone beside which Angel Clare stood with Liza-Lu, waiting "in paralysed suspense" for the final signal. But trees have grown up in later years, and it is not possible to obtain from that point now the view that was obtainable at the time of the novel – except in portions – but an approximate view can be seen from another point, a little to the westward, of "the broad cathedral tower," and the other particular features described in the text.

For the same reason one cannot behold from the milestone – at least, one could not when the present writer was there – the "large red-brick building, with level grey roofs, and rows of short, barred windows bespeaking captivity" in which "justice was done, and the President of the Immortals (in Aeschylean phrase) had ended his sport with Tess." Perhaps Nature's screening is well.

[1] It should be noted that, owing to a mistake in the printing, this has, in most editions, appeared as the *right* hand.

The Gateway, Basing House
(The House of Long-sieging)
The wayfarer in "My Cicely" (*Wessex Poems*) passes this ruin, once a famous mansion.

Remains of Cerne Abbey

My Cicely

"The ancient West Highway" refers to the old Roman Road leading from London to Exeter. Let us follow the wayfarer in imagination. First we hear of him passing "The House of Long-sieging." This, the well-known Basing House, near the village of Old Basing, is now in complete ruin, but was once a famous mansion. During the time of the first Civil War it was fortified for the king by John Paulett, who is said to have engraved the words *Aimez Loyauté* on every pane of glass in the house. It stood a succession of blockades between 1643 and 1645, and on the 14th of October in the latter year it was stormed by Oliver Cromwell himself. During the attack it caught fire and was burned down, the very ruins being razed by order of the Parliament. There is little now to mark its existence except a portion of the gateway and some interior walls.

Next, the rider is said to come in sight of Salisbury Cathedral, disguised as the fair fane of "Poore's olden Episcopal See." "The Stour-bordered Forum," through which he passes, speaks to us of Blandford with its old-time market-place. It is the *Shottsford-Forum* of the novels. *Weatherbury Castle*, another wayside object, comes before us in the novel entitled "Two on a Tower" [Volume 2] where it forms part of a composite scene. Thence he passes through *Casterbridge*, in sight of *Maidon* – the finest earthwork in this country – until he reaches "The Hill-fortress of Eggar," and leaves "Square Pummerie" (Poundbury Camp) to the north. In *Eggar* we recognise Eggardon, another fine example of British earth-castles with an almost impregnable position, and commanding a wide outlook over the surrounding country. In due course he reaches *Exonbury* – a city practically conterminous with Exeter. "The famed Lions-Three" stands about ten miles back from the city on the Taunton Road.

The Lost Pyx

Cerne Abbas, under its slight disguise of *Abbot's Cernel*, figures as the first locality in this poem. It is inside the ancient abbey that the priest is imagined to see his first vision.

Cernel's Abbey was at one time in a thriving condition, but little remains to-day to testify to its vigour, though it might be reconstructed from the numerous fragments of mouldings scattered about. It is said to have been founded by Alwald to commemorate his brother, St. Edmund the Martyr, once king of East Anglia. The gate-house, bearing the shields of the Earl of Cornwall, the Abbey Barn, and certain features in the Abbey House and outbuildings

Porch of Abbott's lodging, Cerne Abbas
"'Ere Cernel Abbey ceased hereabout there dwelt a priest" – the hero of the poem, "The Lost Pyx", was priest and later sub-prior at Cerne Abbey. The porch of the Abbot's Lodging is shown here. The poem is a marvellous solution to the origins of the "cross-in-hand", pictured on page 36.

alone remain as reminiscences of the past. Cerne bears the imprint of having been once a busy town, and history assures us that it was at one time quite a considerable place, containing tanneries and a brewery of no mean size. It used to be celebrated as the dearest-rented place in all Dorset. The church is Perpendicular, with a fine tower and an interesting wood screen kept in fair preservation. On a hill-side close to the village is the "Cerne Giant," a rudely cut figure nearly two hundred feet in length, and of what origin we have no accurate knowledge. Many are the legendary stories attaching to it, and various superstitions still linger in the neighbourhood in connection therewith. Perhaps the most popular theory is that in mediaeval times a giant did actually live in the district, and frequently raided the farmers' stockyards in the adjoining Blackmoor Vale; that on one occasion, after an exceptionaly heavy repast, he lay down to sleep on the hill-side, where the villagers discovered him, fastened him to the ground with ropes and pegs, and then slew him and traced his outline by cutting away the grass. By most antiquarians it is thought to represent the work of mediaeval monks from the abbey below; but probably its origin is in a more remote past. A small earthwork near the church is attributed to Celtic residence.

In imagination we may picture the priest rising up and starting forth to shrive the dying man, struggling through the storm until he reaches the spot called Cross-in-Hand. Of all weird, lonesome spots few can compete with the bleak hill-top whereon this mysterious pillar rears itself from the grassy downland. Its origin is as unknown as that of the Giant of Cerne. It may have been a cross, possessed of sacred significance; it may have represented a boundary mark; or, as others affirm, it may have been a pagan monument. Locally it is also called Crossy-hand, from the fact that the figure of a woman with her hands crossed was once discernible. But all signs of carving have become obliterated now, and not a vestige remains of the basin which once crowned its apex.

The present topographer was informed by an old gipsy woman that it was a wishing-stone, and that any individual who placed his hand upon the stone and registered a wish would invariably find it come true. There were certain conditions necessary, and certain precautions to be taken, but into these we must not enter now. Suffice it that this has been put to the test on more than one occasion, with results that fully justified the gipsy woman's prediction. Absence of accurate knowledge is often termed superstition – there we will leave the matter.

This stone comes before us when we follow Tess on her

Cerne Abbas

journey from *Flintcomb-Ash* to *Emminster* and back, on which occasion she is represented as swearing an oath with her hand on the stone at Alec d'Urberville's dictation. From the vicinity of the stone there spreads out before us a wide view, embracing almost the whole of the Blackmoor Vale, with, in clear weather, a glimpse of the Bristol Channel as well as the English Channel. High-Stoy, Bubb-Down, and other landmarks are visible, and beneath us nestle the hamlets and villages known in "The Woodlanders" as the *Hintocks*. The spot may be reached by taking the road leading from Minterne to Evershot, or by a drive in the contrary direction from Evershot station.

Tess's Lament

Here we are recalled to the time when Tess and Angel Clare parted, after their mutual confession regarding the past. There is the atmosphere of the valley of the Froom, where lie the "Great Dairies," and amongst them *Talbothays*, where she sojourned for so long, and whither her mind now turned with regretful longing. But we have already explored this section of the country when viewing the backgrounds against which the several scenes in Tess's life-history stand out – the whole story is vividly recalled to our mind by the verses now before us.

THE COUNTRY OF

"JUDE THE OBSCURE"

The tract of country which we shall now examine is in the northern portion of Wessex, and as we endeavour to trace the footsteps of Jude from *Marygreen* to *Christminster*, and then to *Melchester* and *Shaston*, and ultimately back to the last scenes of his life at *Christminster*, we shall come upon many spots which only concern us in this one story. Since it was the last written of the Wessex Novels we shall naturally expect to find various towns that form models for the backgrounds less altered than is the case in some of the earlier stories, and this expectation will not be disappointed. The striking similitude which we shall note as existing between the places described to us in the book and the real places which we shall visit makes us very liable to err, and to declare that this or that fictitious place is actually the place we are examining. The feeling is even more strongly forced upon us when trying to elucidate the scenery connected with Jude's history than with any other volume of the series, and so accentuated is the impression that when we come upon the grass-patch at *Marygreen*, five miles south from Wantage, it would require very little imagination to think of the characters as real people who had actually lived and had their being there. In fact, we may find ourselves saying, "Here is the place, but where is Jude?"

To examine the arenas of action as they succeed each other in chronological sequence: The story opens at *Marygreen*, and if we would find the spot which seems to answer to the description given we must go to the downland of southern Berkshire, where by dint of much climbing up and across the hills we shall at length come to the quiet village of Great Fawley, set deeply amidst the undulations of a sparsely populated district, where the cultured land has been wrested from the wild at great pains on the part of the reclaimers. The name of the place at once arrests our attention as providing Jude with his surname, a plan of our author's which is by no means unusual with him.

In July the downs are gay with their carpeting of flowers; the roads which bisect the huge tract of grassland are white, glaringly white in the sunlight, and the impalpable pallid dust of the chalky soil rises freely at the

The Well, Great Fawley
(Marygreen)
"The well . . . was as ancient as the village itself." This well, photographed at the margin of the Green, has since disappeared; another exists, but is covered by the lid of a tomb.

Jude's Progress to Oxford

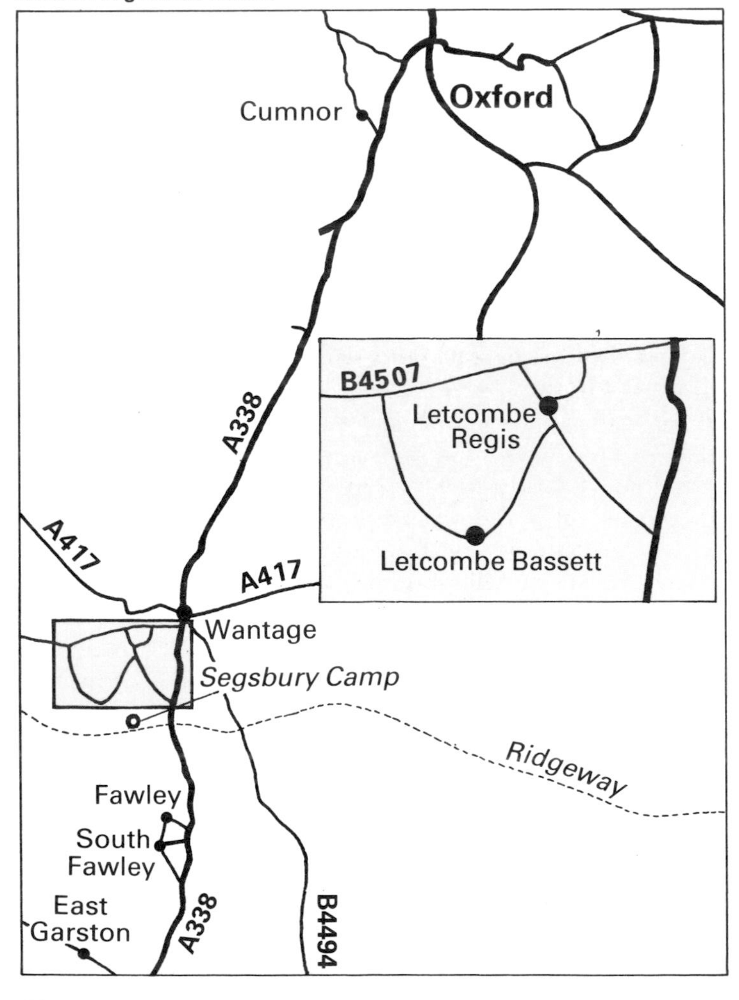

slightest hint of a breeze. Great Fawley is great only in comparison to its lesser neighbour Little Fawley, for in itself it is but a hamlet. If we make our way to the upper part of the village we soon step upon the Green. Near its margin is an old well; here is a school-house; there stands the church; and yonder is a cottage. We have to pull ourselves up smartly, or we shall be declaring positively that *Marygreen* is before our eyes, instead of only the place it symbolises. From the Green we can catch a glimpse of the *Brown House*– known locally as the Red House – with the long stretch of cultivated land sloping up to it.

It is here, at *Marygreen*, that Jude is supposed to have passed the early years of his life, in toil that jarred on his sensitive nature and in circumstances that handicapped him at every turn in his struggle to attain to his ideal, to reach *Christminster*, that city of perfection where the tree of knowledge flourished – far to the northward beyond the hills that encompassed the village and shut it in from the outside world. In imagination we see Jude taking his first step towards his emancipation when he climbs the hill until he reaches the high road at its junction with the old ridgeway, "the Icknield Street and original Roman Road through the district." The old trackway, now entirely grass-grown, is still plainly visible, stretching across the downs until it seems to merge into them and lose its identity. Reaching this spot, Jude was close to the *Brown House*, and by mounting a ladder which stood against it he was able to see in the sky to the northward the halo of light which hung over *Christminster* – virtually Oxford. The high road running eastward still forms the dividing line which separates the cultivated arable land from the natural downland, just as it did when Jude's history was being unfolded to us.

A wide and magnificent view is before us on every hand at the summit of the hill, and a point which cannot fail to strike the beholder is its aloofness from sophistication, and the untrammelled nature of all the surroundings. Surely the environment is aptly chosen, for it would be in just such natural conditions that we should expect a highly–strung and somewhat romantic nature like that of Jude to develop along the lines described, imbibing strange, perhaps weird, ideas regarding life; the common-place things of every day assuming proportions greater than they really bore. There is much ancient history shut up within these hills, leading the most prosaic mind to speculate on the peoples of a bygone age who moved amongst them and had their being in the midst of these Berkshire wildernesses.

Alfredston (potentially Wantage) now claims our atten-

The Cottage at Letcombe Bassett *(Cresscombe)*
Here at Letcombe Bassett was the cottage home of Arabella and her parents.

Jude's Oxford

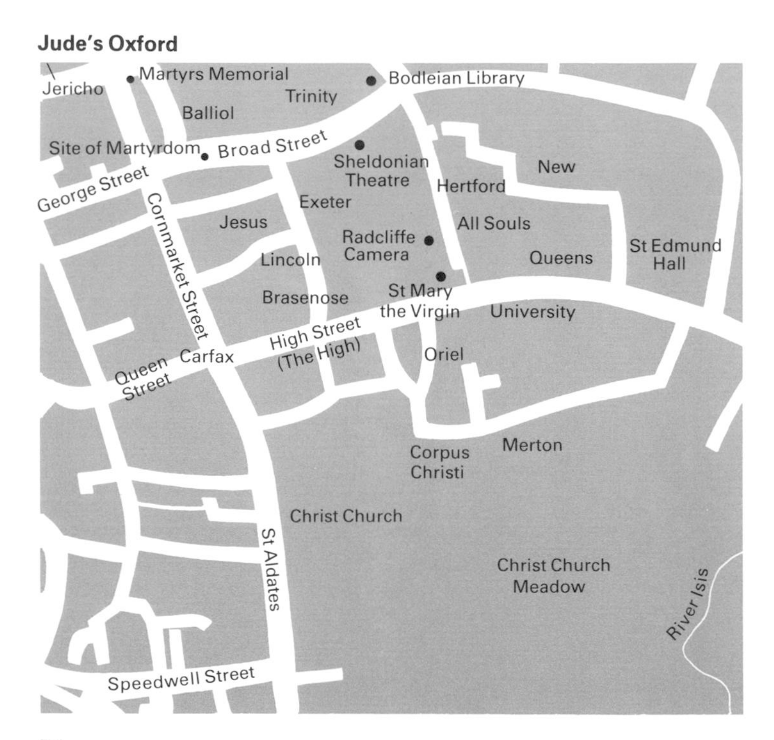

tion, for it was here that Jude went for a time as apprentice to a stone-cutter. To students of the Wessex country Wantage is interesting as being the birthplace of King Alfred in 849, for to him is due much of the credit of making Wessex what it is. In the centre of the market-place stands a large statue to his memory. The origin of its fictitious name becomes clear to us when we realise the connection of the place with the old Wessex ruler. Other than the town itself as a whole there is little detail to claim us, and we soon turn our steps towards *Cresscombe*.

A clue is given to its position in regard to Wantage and Great Fawley, and when our search takes us to the little village of Letcombe Bassett we quickly realise its close approximation to the *Cresscombe* of the story. It is a rough track thither from Great Fawley and difficult to find, but the village is easily reached from Wantage by the direct road. After we strike the river and follow beside it for a short while we come upon a picturesque thatched cottage standing right among the watercress beds; and again we see the appositeness of its coined name. The cottage seems somehow familiar to us, and it does not require much stretch of fancy to picture Arabella and her happy-go-lucky parents as its once inhabitants, so good a model is it for our author's description. Here, at *Cresscombe*, was the first and odd meeting of Jude and Arabella, a meeting destined to colour the whole of his future life.

Before we leave this vicinity to discover the next back-scene we shall naturally wish to find that "lonely roadside cottage between the Brown House and Marygreen," where Jude lived after his marriage. But here we meet with disappointment; real as it has been and as it is remembered – starved fir-tees and all – it was completely destroyed by fire some twenty years ago, and only the site on which it stood can now be pointed out by the local residents.

If we follow in Jude's wake we shall come to *Christminster* in about fifteen miles. A greater contrast than that offered between the calm isolation of *Marygreen* and the thronged streets of *Christminster* it would be hard to imagine. We see Jude making his way thither with hope beating strongly in his heart. "He now paused at the top of a crooked and gentle declivity, and obtained his first near view of the city. Grey-stoned and dun-roofed, it stood within hail of the Wessex border." The action proceeds here for a considerable time; it is at *Christminster*, the city of his dreams, that Jude learns some of the bitterest lessons of life. Of the fact that Oxford provided our author with an outline from which was painted *Christminster* we can have but little doubt; many of the individual features

The School-house, Cumnor *(Lumsdon)*
The old school-house remains, albeit not in use as the main school.

Porch of St Mary-the-Virgin, Oxford *(Christminster)*
Lea explored the many intriguing real locations at four o'clock one morning when the streets were, understandably, deserted. St Mary-the-Virgin is "the Church with the Italian Porch".

mentioned are recognisable at a glance, and we need have no compunction in claiming the correlation.

It was at four o'clock one morning, when the streets were entirely deserted, that the present writer started to explore the city with a view of identifying the real with the artificial – a time of day eminently suited to the purpose. Perhaps High Street may seem familiar to us as *Chief Street*; Merton Street with its cobbled paving, as the equivalent of *Old Time Street*; Carfax is undeniably the begetter of *Four Ways*; Christ Church brings *Cardinal College* to our minds; while Corpus Christi, or New, is substantially *Sarcophagus*. There can be no doubt that the Church of St. Mary-the-Virgin is identical with "the Church with the Italian Porch"; nor need we hesitate to discern in the Sheldonian Theatre, "the circular theatre with that well-known lantern above it," one of Wren's masterpieces, and more or less suggested by the ancient theatre of Marcellus at Rome.

With these features before us we shall find little difficulty in following Jude and the other characters as they move across the stage at *Christminster*. To attempt any adequate description of the town and its architecture would occupy far more space than need be allotted here; all such particulars can be gleaned from the various histories and guides readily obtainable. Here Jude first met Sue – at the ominous spot in Broad Street where the Martyrs were burnt. The cross in the pavement marks it still.

Shortly after we first became interested in *Christminster* we renew acquaintance with Phillotson in the school-house at *Lumsdon*. If we go to the village of Cumnor we shall find the original school-house from which Phillotson's residence was more or less drawn. No specially important episodes take place here, and our attention is soon diverted to an examination of that city of which the counterfeit name is *Melchester*.

We have already decided in a former chapter ("Tess") that for the purposes of our idle wandering, Salisbury may be taken to represent *Melchester*. It would be easy to write volumes on the history of this ancient city, but it must suffice us now to examine only such individual features as occur in the story. It is here that Sue is supposed to come when she joins the "Melchester Normal School." The building which suggested the school is still a training college, and stands just outside the Close facing the western end of the Cathedral. The back of the house gives ready access to the river by passing down the length of the garden. "It was an ancient edifice of the fifteenth century, once a palace, now a training school, with mullioned and

Salisbury Cathedral *(Melchester Cathedral)*
The cathedral of the story *On the Western Circuit* and the poem "My Cicely", as well as of *Jude the Obscure*. Jude "walked out into the dull winter light over the town bridge, and turned the corner towards the Close. The day was foggy, and standing under the walls of the most graceful architectural pile in England, he paused and looked up."

Salisbury *("Melchester Normal School")*
"It was an ancient edifice of the fifteenth century, once a palace, now a training school, with mullioned and transomed windows." The Teachers' Training College, which was the *Melchester Normal School* attended by Sue, has been closed and the building enlarged.

The Market-house, Salisbury *(Melchester)*
This is also the scene of the meeting of Raye and Anna *On the Western Circuit* (*Life's Little Ironies*). It has now been replaced by the new City Library.

transomed windows, and a courtyard in front shut in from the road by a wall" – thus our author. And if we choose to compare his description with the original we shall find it exact, saving in one or two minor details. The wall is now represented by iron railings, and the courtyard has been transformed into a lawn. The old building is honoured with the ghost of the murdered Duke of Buckingham – a cause of creepiness at nights to the threescore young women in training there.

Very soon after Sue's arrival Jude takes up his quarters in the town, where he is said to have quickly obtained the work on which he had set his heart – "the Cathedral repairs." (The building was restored by Sir Gilbert Scott between 1870 and 1880, and many workmen employed.) *Melchester* Cathedral, "the most graceful architectural pile in England," figures in several of the Wessex Novels, but is too well known to need any elaborate description here. Besides the Cathedral and its Close, our attention is further claimed by the North Gate leading into High Street; the Market-house, and the "Grey Perpendicular Church of St. Thomas" in which Sue's marriage with Phillotson is supposed to have taken place. These, figuring under their real names, are easily studied.

From whichever direction we approach Salisbury, the spire of the Cathedral – the highest in the country – forces itself upon our view long before we become aware of human habitations. The town carries within itself an old-world atmosphere which is strongly intensified on market days by the presence of the country people who flock in from the surrounding villages, and by the snatches of dialect which break forth on all sides as we pass through the thronged market-square.

We are led to regard it as a day of much importance when Jude and Sue spend their holiday in visiting Wardour Castle – figuring under its rightful name. To the archaeologist the somewhat severe Corinthian building is less interesting than the old castle near, surrounded by its magnificent trees, but now in utter ruin. The chief interest in the more modern building lies in its picture-galleries, well known to most lovers of art, and marked by the preponderance of the Italian School. We cannot locate definitely the cottage in which the weetless pair are said to have stayed the night, though we may surmise that it lay near Chicklade Ridge or Chilmark Down, in the direction of Wylye Station, from which place or Cadford they had intended to take train.

The *Kennetbridge* of the story suggests Newbury. Here lived the composer of the hymn that so haunted Jude; his journey thither, and the sense of disappointment with the

Old Grove's Place, Shaftesbury
(Shaston)
This building "occupies nearly the position which is assigned in an old map of Shaftesbury to the habitation of one Mr Groves; hence the name" (B. C. A. Windle). This remains very much the same, today, though were Sue and Phillotson to revisit it, they would discover a certain amount of re-design both inside and out.

Jude's Shaftesbury

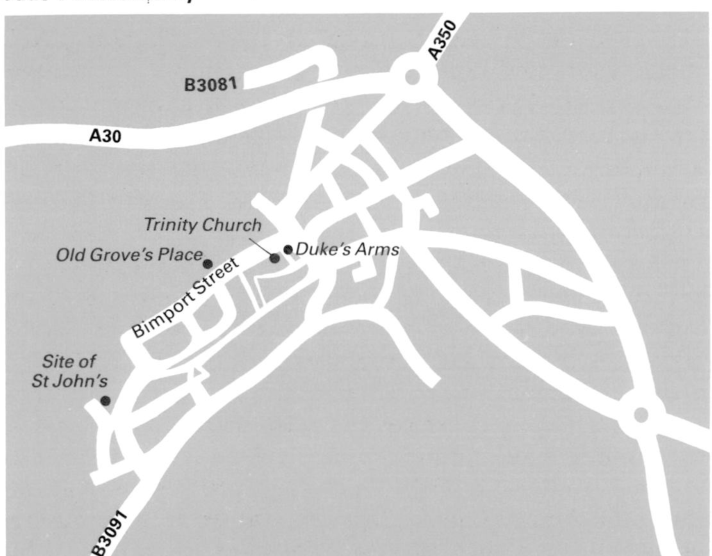

man which it brought, forms an incisive episode in Jude's career.

The action now shifts to *Shaston* (typical of Shaftesbury). "The ancient British Palladour . . . was, and is, in itself the city of a dream," says our author. If we compare the description given in the book with the effect which is produced on us by a ramble through the town, we shall be struck with the exactness of his delineation. There is, of course, to-day the incongruous blending of the old and the new, but under the veneer of modern transmutations consequent on a spirit of commercialism we can still appreciate its ancient historic interests. "Vague imaginings of its castle, its three mints, its magnificent apsidal Abbey, the chief glory of South Wessex, its twelve churches, its shrines, chantries, hospitals . . . – all now ruthlessly swept away – throw the visitor, even against his will, into a pensive melancholy . . . ." Yes, *Shaston* – a historic contraction of Shaftesbury, by the way – to-day shows us but the skeleton of what it was in the Middle Ages, and there is a spirit of iconoclasm still at work which must, alas, result in further degradation to the ancient features of the old town.

Its position, raised high above the encompassing Blackmoor Vale, gives it an imposing appearance, and from it extends a superb view into the adjoining counties. From whatever direction the wind may blow, it smites the town with a vigour that threatens to sweep it from off its pedestal. "It was to this breezy and whimsical spot that Jude ascended" when he came to visit Sue, now Mrs. Phillotson, at the school-house. They lived in the house known as Old-Grove or "Old Grove's-Place," still to be seen standing almost opposite the school. The building dates back to the early part of the sixteenth century, and contains some interesting wood-carving. The "Abbey Walk" passes in front of the school, and leads towards the walls that face south. Of the Abbey itself, attached to what was perhaps the wealthiest nunnery in the country, nothing remains except the ruins of the walls which enclosed it, although the foundations of the Abbey Church and other relics are to be seen. Other features which receive cursory notice are the Duke's Arms Hotel in the Market Place, Bimport Street, and "the venerable graveyard of Trinity Church, with its avenues of limes," presented under their actual names.

Although there are traces of British and Roman occupation in the immediate neighbourhood, Shaftesbury has no history anterior to Saxon times, when it was a place of considerable importance. Legendary accounts connect the town with the date of King Solomon. Together with

The George Hotel, Reading
(Aldbrickham)
The hotel where Jude and Sue stayed, and where Jude had earlier become reconciled with Arabella, remains one of the better hotels in the town.

Dorchester, Bridport, and Wareham, it formed one of the four royal boroughs of Dorset. The industries carried on in the town in the seventeenth century – the manufacturers of leather, worsteds, and buttons – have now completely died out.

For a brief space our characters are back at *Marygreen*, where we read of Jude's alienation from orthodoxy and the burning of his once treasured possessions: "Jeremy Taylor, Butler, Doddridge, Paley, Newman and the rest had gone to ashes."

This alteration in his principles comes almost concomitantly with that in Sue's, which now leads her to entreat Phillotson to sanction her leaving him and joining Jude. As the direct result of this request we picture him going to *Leddenton* to confer with his friend Gillingham. "Leaving Duncliffe Hill on the left . . . he crossed a tributary of the Stour, and reached Leddenton." It would seem to accord with the little town of Gillingham washed by the river Leddon, or Loddon, the friend's name giving us a further clue to the identity of the place. To this townlet there is no other interest attaching.

It seems impossible to conjure up any spark of romanticism in regard to that eminently commercial town Reading. Yet it is an old town, and it is there that we must turn in order to follow the queer pair. *Aldbrickham* was doubtless drawn from Reading. It is essentially a place of progress, of constant alterations, whereby most of its ancient interests have become entirely shrouded by the present up-to-dateness. We find it impossible to locate the house in which Jude and Sue lived so long, and where he carried on his work as a monumental mason. There are hundreds of such houses in such streets. The George Hotel is easily discovered, however.

Stoke-Barehills – symbolising Basingstoke – is our next platform. It is an ancient place, and was once in occupation by the Romans, but here, too, we find with regret extensive alterations. Our author says of it: "It stands with its gaunt, unattractive, ancient church, and its new red-brick suburb, amid the open chalk-soiled cornlands. The most familiar object in Stoke-Barehills nowadays is its cemetery, standing among some picturesque mediaeval ruins beside the railway . . . " The mediaeval ruins referred to are all that remains of the chapel of the Holy Ghost. It was founded in 1525, but in less than a century it lost its renown. Jude is supposed to have taken Sue and the boy to Basingstoke to see the agricultural show, when they were recognised by Arabella and her husband.

There is no distinctive name given to the church at which Jude and Sue were working as decorators, and the

View from Carfax, Oxford *(Four Ways)*

only guide we have to its position is the indication that it lay some two miles out of the town and at no great distance from the village of *Gaymead*. This village, as well as the town of *Aldbrickham*, comes before us again in the story entitled "The Son's Veto" – one of "Life's Little Ironies," – and there we identify it as the fictitious presentment of Shinfield, a village lying a few miles to the south of Reading. Jude's discharge from his work at this church marks the declination of their fortunes, and from that time there commenced for them a "shifting, almost nomadic, life." Their wandering from place to place in search of work lasted for two years and a half, when we read of him "shaping the mullions of a country mansion, sometimes setting the parapet of a town-hall, sometimes ashlaring an hotel at Sandbourne (Bournemouth), sometimes a museum at Casterbridge (Dorchester), sometimes as far down as Exonbury (Exeter), sometimes at Stoke-Barehills (Basingstoke). Later still he was at Kennetbridge (Newbury) . . . ." It is at this last place that Arabella comes again on the stage, and finds Sue selling cakes at a stall in the fair.

Our interest now reverts to *Christminster*. Here, in the temporary lodging, that gruesome scene – the hanging of the children by the boy, Father Time – is supposed to have been enacted. "Done because we are too menny" was the pencilled line he left behind to explain his action. Following closely on this tragedy we learn of the great change which is working in the minds of our two principal characters. Jude's outlook on life now becomes heterodox; Sue's paganism merges into orthodoxy, leading her to enter frequently the church of *St. Silas* for meditation or prayer.

This church was said to be situated in the most populous district of the city, termed *Beersheba*. This gives us a clue to its whereabouts, and a little search shows to us that *Beersheba* is probably a pseudonym of "Jericho," while the church of *St. Silas* is in the likeness of St. Barnabas (designed, by the way, by the late Sir Arthur Blomfield, R. A., with whom our author studied Architecture).

Phillotson is now back at his old school-house at *Marygreen*, and in order to rejoin him Sue goes thither – by train to *Alfredston*, driving near to the village, and walking the remainder of the distance. "She crossed by the well and under the trees to the pretty new school on the other side." The following morning sees them re-married in the new church which stands but a short distance from the school-house.

Immediately following this event we are told of Jude's

The High Street, Oxford *(Chief Street)*

reunion with Arabella. She discovers him in the tavern whereat she was once a barmaid (a place we cannot locate definitely), and aids in making him drunk. Then we see her leading him towards her father's house, passing the Martyr's Cross in Broad Street.

Jude's health now becomes worse. We may track him as he journeys by rail to *Alfredston* and walks the five miles to *Marygreen*. Here he has an interview with Sue in the church, and then we watch him as he retraces his steps, leaving behind him the old familiar footpath which led across "the fields in which he had scared rooks as a boy," on past the *Brown House*, crossing the old Ridgeway, till he comes to the milestone on which he had carved his name so many years before. There he spreads his blanket on the wet ground and stops to rest awhile. "He passed the spot where the gibbet of his ancestor and Sue's had stood, and descended the hill." It is late when he at length reaches *Christminster*. At the station he is met by Arabella, and we see them passing together along the street by "the silent colleges." Reminiscences crowd on him. "This is Old Rubric," he says. "And this Sarcophagus; and up that lane Crozier and Tudor; and all down there is Cardinal with its long front, and its windows with lifted eyebrows." If we pass down St. Aldates's Street we may stand awhile and conjecture which of the colleges before us are most appropriately served by the factitious names our author bestows on them. Certainly we shall not be very wide of the mark in supposing that *Cardinal* is more or less representative of Christ Church, when the others will naturally drop into their respective places.

The action is again at *Marygreen* for the last time; and then *Christminster* holds us for the final scene. It is the death-bed of Jude. The house in which he finally lives, and in which he dies, we cannot find; it was in the central portion of the town and at no great distance from the Sheldonian Theatre. Let that approximation suffice; we have already torn the veil somewhat ruthlessly in our endeavour to discover the real and to make it conterminous with the counterfeit.

The Vampirine Fair

Wingreen Hill is near Salisbury; the *Manor Court* can hardly be other than a fictitious presentment of Rushmore House; and in *Shastonb'ry* we easily recognise Shaftesbury.

THE COUNTRY OF "THE WOODLANDERS"

The country of "The Woodlanders" is the most perplexing of all the topographies in the Wessex Novels. The action takes us to the northern portion of the county of Dorset – or South Wessex as it is termed in these books – on the outskirts of Blackmoor Vale. This district is essentially one of woodlands, interspersed with wide open commons, boggy marshes, and high grassy uplands. It is a region inhabited by simple-minded people, where many old-fashioned ideas and superstitions still linger. With the exception of the two main roads – Dorchester-Sherborne, and Dorchester-Yeovil – all the thoroughfares connecting the villages are little better than lanes, most of them winding, and some passing up and down steep hills. Owing to the heavy nature of the soil, such lanes become muddy and slippery in winter-time; the air is oppressive, and produces on the traveller a curious feeling of lassitude. These factors combine to explain the small amount of traffic and the comparative rarity of intrusion by strangers; they may account also to a large extent for the meagre population, and the prevalence and persistence of unsophisticated thought. Unfortunately, a retrogressive movement is apparent to those who were familiar with the locality thirty or more years ago; many houses and homesteads have fallen into decay and have disappeared; the timber trade, of which we hear so much in the story, has declined, and with it has gone many of the smaller industries which were intimately connected with the larger business – hollow-turning, hurdle-making, the splitting of thatching-spars, and the like.

In some of the Wessex Novels and Poems we can point confidently to this or that as being the actual model from which our author painted his word-picture, but in the present instance it is exceedingly difficult to identify, even approximately, many of the features described. We are told in the preface that the natural configurations are given under their real names; with this to guide us we can gain a fair insight into the position of the actual woodlands; but, in regard to the villages and hamlets, we must content ourselves with conjecture.

The *Hintocks* may be said to embrace Hermitage, Hillfield, Middlemarsh, Minterne, and Melbury Bubb,

High Stoy

A Tour of the Woodlanders Country

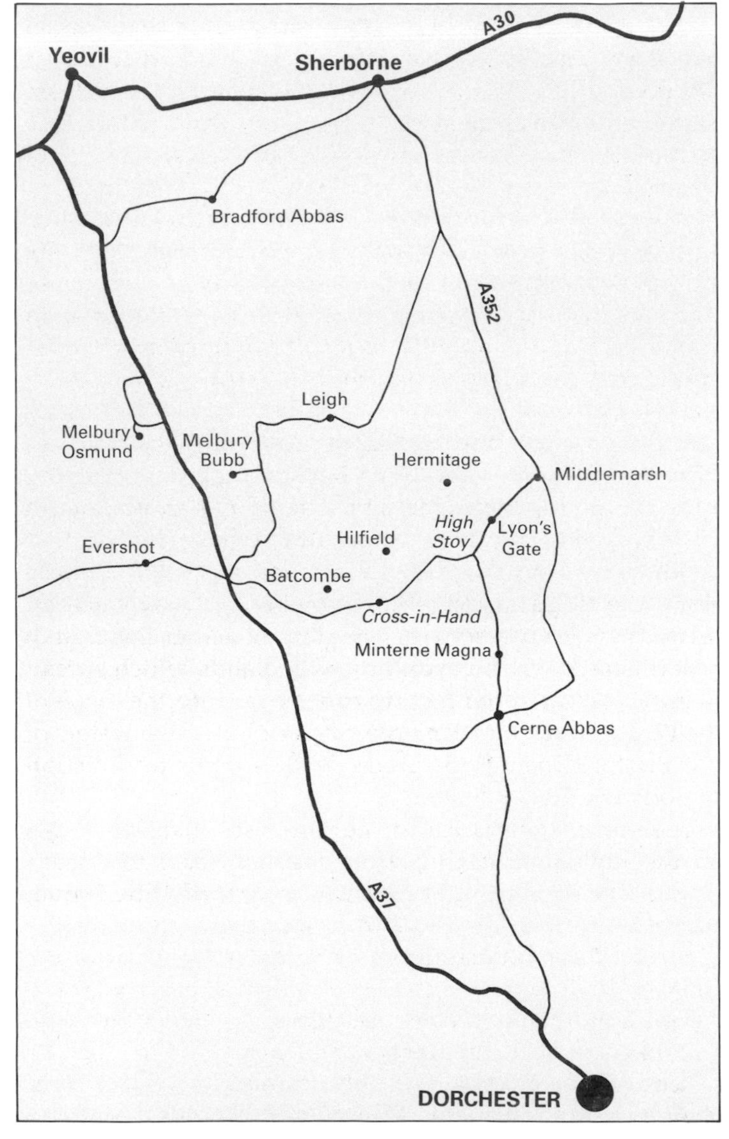

either wholly or in part, as well as certain isolated homesteads and houses. The descriptions in the book would seem to be chosen from one or other of these places without much attempt at exact localisation; and if we choose to regard Minterne as typical of *Great Hintock*, and Hermitage as exemplified in *Little Hintock*, it must be with a certain amount of diffidence and an acknowledgment that these designations are by no means arbitrary. We shall search in vain for Melbury's homestead; for the cottage that sheltered Marty South; for the house where Fitzpiers lived; for the home of Giles Winterborne. Time had done its work too thoroughly in this direction. The woodlands themselves have altered in appearance; the full-grown timber-tree of to-day was a mere sapling at the time the story was written; what was mature timber then has long been converted into planks, and distributed hither and thither; some of the old plantations have been rooted and transformed into agricultural land, while new plantations have sprung up as substitutes. But, in spite of these many changes, we can still allow our imaginations rein when we stand among the woodlands to-day and gaze at the mature oaks, or the sapling beeches, or the struggling seedlings, and for the moment we may lose count of time and mentallly reconstruct the scenes in which figured the familiar forms of Melbury, and Grace, and Marty South, and Winterborne, as they played their allotted parts.

We may spend many pleasant days in the country of "The Woodlanders," rambling here and there, journeying from village to village, taking the footpaths in preference to the roads, trying to conjecture where this or that incident was supposed to have taken place; or walking along the ridge of High-Stoy, whence we may catch an occasional glimpse between the trees of a house or church or farmstead; while beyond the woodlands which spread themselves out at our feet we can see far into the "Vale of the White Hart," and even can catch a glint of the waters of the Bristol Channel. In precisely the opposite direction spreads the distant Solent.

The scenery on which the curtain rises displays a spot on the high road leading from *Sherton Abbas* to *Abbot's Cernel*. The former of these places is virtually Sherborne; the latter Cerne Abbas. At this particular point on the highway Barber Percomb stops to inquire his way to *Little Hintock*. If we follow the directions which are given him we shall come to the hamlet of Hermitage. High-Stoy Hill had been visible to him for some miles back on the road he had travelled. It rears itself out of the valley on our right hand as we face Minterne – Dogbury Hill being on our left

Hermitage Church *(Little Hintock Church)*
This, like the church of Melbury Bubb, which was also drawn upon by Hardy in his description of *Little Hintock Church*, survives today.

Revels Inn Farm, Middlemarsh *(Revellers Inn)*
There are still a few relics (including the glass door mentioned by Lea) to connect Revels Inn Farm with *Revellers Inn*, "whither Tim and Suke and the wedding party were bound when Fitzpiers met them."

hand – and forms a landmark visible, and easily recognised, from long distances, a fact owing partly to its shape and partly to its altitude. The hill commands an extensive view over the vale below, and we shall have occasion to refer to it repeatedly in following the course of "The Woodlanders'" history. The serpentine road which ascends out of Lion's Gate village is the same as that which Fitzpiers and Grace are supposed to have climbed when the former was on his way to visit Mrs. Charmond at *Middleton Abbey*. After they parted, Grace "ascended the slope of High-Stoy and watched his descent. . . . His way was east. . . ." The same two characters come before us again at the summit of this hill when, after their separation, Fitzpiers begs Grace to grant him an interview.

The actual house which formed the model for *Great Hintock House*, and which was supposed to have stood at no great distance from *Little Hintock*, has been swept away since the date at which the characters were imagined to have lived. It has been stated that the house had a reality in Upcerne House – a delightful Tudor mansion standing on the south side of Batcombe Down – but although certain features in the description may have been taken from this house, we cannot consider it typical, either in regard to its architecture or its situation.

The church, with the adjoining graveyard in which Giles Winterborne was supposedly interred, was a composite structure, drawn in part from the church of Melbury Bubb, as well as from that of Hermitage – which more nearly represents its position.

Some details certainly suggest Middlemarsh. Here we are concerned in a search for *Revellers Inn*, whither Tim and Suke and the wedding party were bound when Fitzpiers met them. "Just walking round the parishes to show ourselves a bit," was their explanation to him. This inn was once a posting-house of no mean size, but is now a farm-house and passes by the name of Revels Farm. It is an old building and possesses certain suggestive features reminding us of its former employment. In what was once the bar we may see the money-till underneath a bench-table with a well-worn slot in it, through which the coins were dropped. Connecting the bar-room with the old kitchen is a glass door with curious latticed panes of bottle-glass.

We will now glance at the places outside the boundary of the *Hintock* country. *Middleton Abbey* is mentioned as the temporary residence of Mrs. Charmond. The abbey at Milton Abbas seems to have suggested it to our author. We find an interesting village, built on model lines; all the

The Abbey at Milton Abbas
(Middleton Abbey)
The abbey above is situated at Milton Abbas and is the inspiration for Middleton Abbey. "They walked about the Abbey aisles."

The Digby Hotel, Sherborne
(The Earl of Wessex, Sherton Abbas)
The building still stands, though it is no longer a hotel and has been acquired for use by Sherborne School.

houses on both sides of the long wide street are almost exactly similar in size and design, and all are roofed with thatch. There used to be a magnificent avenue of chestnut trees, but these were pollarded a year or two ago because of the dampness caused by their over-hanging branches; they are beginning to recover themselves, however, and in a few years we may again see the grand display of blossom which made the village so conspicuous. The fine old abbey, which gives the place part of its name, comes as a sudden surprise to the traveller, for among the quiet rural surroundings we little expect to see this ancient building of Saxon foundation. Close beside the abbey-church stands the house which was doubtless imagined as the place of Mrs. Charmond's sojourn.

The village of *Oakbury Fitzpiers*, which Melbury pointed out to Grace as being the ancient home of the Fitzpiers family, seems to us to be represented in Okeford Fitzpaine, a village lying in the valley of the Stour in the direction of Blandford – a town which appears more or less identical with the *Shottsford-Forum* of the story.

Sherton Abbas, the fascinating old town full of quaint bits of architecture and mediaeval buildings, comes before us as an approximation of Sherborne. The market-place, right in the centre of the town, is where we picture Giles Winterborne standing under his specimen apple-tree, close to the sixteenth-century conduit, which was placed there after its removal from the cloisters of the abbey. The Digby Hotel seems to answer to the "Earl of Wessex"; but the "Three Tuns," a hostel of much less importance, must have been drawn from one of the many inns which have disappeared of late years. A visit to the abbey-church will bring back to us the day when Grace and Giles went there, "walked about the abbey aisles and presently sat down." The abbey-church displays to us many distinct periods in its architecture – Norman, Early English, Decorated, and Perpendicular. From the year 705 to 1075 Sherborne was the seat of a bishopric which included Dorset, Somerset, and part of Wilts and Devon.

Sherborne is a delightfully situated old-world town, surrounded by high hills from which we may see some panoramic views of the neighbourhood that include many landscapes interesting to the Hardy reader. On market days the little town is very busy and the streets are crowded; but on other days it exhibits an attitude towards strangers which can only be termed as "sleepy." Among the many interesting buildings is the school; in the museum attached to it we shall find the noted megalosaurus, whose upper and lower jaws are more perfect than any other specimen extant. With the old castle we shall

The Market Place, Sherborne
(Sherton Abbas)
Where Giles Winterborne is discovered "standing, as he always did at this season of the year, with his specimen apple tree."

deal later, when it serves as the background for "Anna Lady Baxby," in "A Group of Noble Dames."

The final scene takes us back to the churchyard of *Little Hintock* and "a motionless figure standing by the gate." Marty South is pictured visiting the grave of Giles Winterborne. But there is no stone marking the spot, no clue to guide us in our search, and we must leave the country of "The Woodlanders" with the frank admission that we have not discovered as much as we could wish.

The Home-Coming

The scenery here is peculiarly appropriate to the theme of the poem. Toller Down was chosen by our author with due regard to effect. It is a lonesome spot, quite sufficient in itself to explain the utter feeling of isolation which gripped the bride on her introduction to the wind-swept upland. Coming thither from *Ivel* (*i.e.* Yeovil) the contrast is further impressed. If we visit Toller Down in the autumn or winter we shall have little difficulty in proving to ourselves the truth contained in our author's description of the spot. The boisterous wind, howling, driving before it everything movable, cutting like a knife over the ridges, forming a concentrated draught through the valleys and cuttings, hurries away down "Crimmercrock's long lane" – the road leading from Maiden Newton to Rampisham – still so called.

The Impercipient

It was during a service in Salisbury Cathedral that our author was impressed and inspired to compare the various thoughts that seemed to echo through the aisles. When we were examining the backgrounds in "Jude the Obscure" we inspected the Cathedral more closely.

At an Inn

At the George Inn at Winchester these verses were written; but beyond stating this as a crude fact there is nothing further to dilate on.

The Slow Nature

This poem brings the Froom Valley before our eyes – the valley which occurs so often as a background in "Tess of the d'Urbervilles." In *Moreford Rise* we find a fictitious presentment of a hill close to Moreton Village, in the direction of Winfrith. "Far Egdon-side" and "the rippling Froom" indicate at once a locality not remote from *Talbothays*.

Marshall's Elm
Today's owners offer bed and breakfast. There are few outward signs of change except that the verandah roof seen in Lea's picture has been removed (the mark of its position is still visible on the outside of the building). This is the location of the murder in "A Trampwoman's Tragedy".

San Sebastian

"San Sebastian" has for its setting the *Ivel Way*, that old Roman road which led through Bath until it reached Ilchester, where it branched through Yeovil to Dorchester, and on the other fork led to Exeter. There is a reference to the *Hintock Maypole*, which brings our minds back to the story of "The Woodlanders." Maypole-dancing is now almost extinct, though an occasional Wessex village may be seen where the Maypole still rears itself on the green – notably at the village of Shillingstone, between Wimborne and Blandford. Round-the-Maypole was once one of the most popular of the Morris or Moorish dances, and was introduced into England from Spain in the time of Edward III.

A Trampwoman's Tragedy

If we follow the tracks

> My fancy-man, and jeering John,
> And Mother Lee, and I

took on an eventful day, we shall need to climb some of the greatest heights of western Wessex and dip down into some of its lowest levels. Such a course will bring before us scenery of exceeding beauty and diversity.

The road which leads from Dorchester to Crewkerne passes through Maiden Newton and climbs Whitesheet Hill. Leaving Crimmercrock Lane on our right hand, and passing Benvill Lane on the top of Toller Down, we soon reach Wynyard's Gap, some three miles from Crewkerne. From here our road is practically due north; we pass "sad Sedge-Moor," climb "the toilsome Poldon crest," and in due course reach Marshall's Elm, the scene of the imagined tragedy. This inn has now become a farm-house, its licence having dropped thirty or more years ago. It stands at the crest of the ridgeway, above the village of the same name, just at the junction of five roads. A wonderful view extends from this point, the moors lying below to the westward, and Glastonbury Tor rising out of the valley northwards. The old swinging sign, bearing a picture of the battle of Sedgemoor, has entirely disappeared, though it is still remembered by some of the older inhabitants.

For months previous the quartette had wandered here and there, in the *Great Forest* – the New Forest, once the chief haunt of gipsy-folk, – through "Blackmoor wide" – the Vale with which Hardy readers are very familiar as "the Vale of the Little Dairies," – crossing the Parret, climbing the Mendips, fording the Yeo – the stream that runs beside the town of Yeovil and gives its name thereto,

Wynyards Gap Inn
This is the "cosy house at Wynyard's Gap" mentioned in "A Trampwoman's Tragedy". It has undergone few changes since Hardy wrote about it.

Windwhistle Inn
Still there today, but recently modernised.

– and thence through the Marshwood Fens.

Some of the "lone inns" visited are still in existence. King's Stag was burnt down about fifteen years ago, and its site is now filled by some modern cottages. Nearly opposite, at the pottery, we may see the post from which its sign depended, but the sign was blown down a short time back; it is still preserved, however, and there is a proposition afoot to have it repaired and erected at the cross-roads close by. The sign depicts the head of a stag with a collar round its neck, and on it is the following doggerel:

> When Julius Caesar reigned here
> I was but then a little deer;
> When Julius Caesar reigned King
> Around my neck he put this ring.
> Whoever doth me overtake,
> Pray spare my life for Caesar's sake.

King's Stag was once famous for its Maypole; the revels started on June 11 and lasted for three days, during which time people flocked from far and near, and the old inn overflowed with visitors to such an extent that many had to be refused accommodation.

Windwhistle Inn – another halting-place of the four characters in the tragedy – stands about four miles from Crewkerne on the road leading to Exeter. It was once a noted posting-house, and still preserves many of its old-time characteristics, including the high-backed settles in the kitchen. It was also famed as a favourite haunt of certain highwaymen; its isolated position no doubt made it an excellent rendezvous. Many stories are still told of the gang who met there. An old well – now foundered in – used to be pointed out as the hiding-place wherein the bodies of the victims were thrown.

"The Horse on Hintock Green" is discoverable in the White Horse at Middlemarsh – one of the villages that go to complete the *Hintocks* of "The Woodlanders". It is a picturesque building of weatherworn brick; the tiled roof is laid to a pattern and the tiles themselves are moss-grown, the chimneys are massive and elaborated with dentil courses under the copings.

"The cozy house at Wynyard's Gap" aforesaid deserves that title to-day; it lies close to the road just after we begin the descent of the hill towards Crewkerne.

The "hut renowned on Bredy Knap" has long ceased to be an inn, though the fabric remains. It is easily discovered on the roadside between Dorchester and Bridport.

It was at *Ivel-chester*, the old name here used for Ilchester, that the hanging is supposed to take place. The

The White Horse Inn, Middlemarsh
This is " 'The Horse' on Hintock Green" in "A Trampwoman's Tragedy".

Woodlanders Country
This photograph appeared as the frontispiece to the Wessex edition of *The Woodlanders*. It is an area in which distances may be "conveniently curtailed by following footpaths", as Lea suggested in an earlier work.

gaol was built in 1188. The town's decadence was perceptibly helped by the introduction of railways, the line leaving Ilchester out of count; but until then it formed a good centre for agricultural trading, situated as it is on the margin of the moors, where vast herds of cattle graze. Its market dates from before the Conquest. The river Yeo or Ivel runs close beside the town, and right on its bank stood the said county gaol. We may still see the hanging-chamber with its balcony, from which the victim was launched forth to swing over the river. Not far from the thriving town of Yeovil, Ilchester is a sleepy, old-world place, saturated with a feeling of restfulness which is not lost on the stranger who visits it. A picturesque cross stands in the market-place, erected to ensure fair dealing between buyer and vendor, and just behind it is the hall wherein numberless prisoners were tried and condemned. Away from the town stretch the wide moors, extending westwards to the Bristol Channel.

Glastonbury, or Glaston Twelve Hides, which also comes into this poem, is a town of absorbing interest to the archaeologist; its Tor, once an island, but now a peninsula hemmed in on three sides by the river Brue, is visible from many miles distant. We must not pause to examine the town in detail, but a few of its main features may be enumerated. The abbot's kitchen – practically all that remains of the domestic part of the once famous abbey – is a curious and unique building; outside the walls are square, the inside is octagonal, and the corners are filled in with fireplaces and chimneys. The Chapel of St. Joseph is transitional work of the twelfth century. The Great Church, the longest in the whole country, measured 140 feet from east to west, and was 80 feet in width in the nave. The Glastonbury Thorn is supposed to have been planted by Joseph of Arimathea, who, on his arrival, stuck his staff into the ground; it took root and grew, and is said to be a distinct variety, flowering twice a year.

Many and interesting are the legends associated with Glastonbury, one of the most curious being that Joseph of Arimathea, the leader of twelve apostles sent from Gaul by St. Philip, erected the first church here, a small wattled building. From early times, and through the Middle Ages, it was the scene of many pilgrimages.

The Pine Planters

Here is the country of "The Woodlanders" before us once more. No particular spot is mentioned, but such detail seems scarcely necessary. We have thoroughly explored this country and the *Hintock* villages and hamlets, and the poem interests us more as a reminder of the book in question than as one which breaks fresh ground for topographical research.

In a Wood

If we ramble through the *Hintock Woods,* familiar to us in the book entitled the "The Woodlanders," we shall find the country which formed the setting for this poem.

"LIFE'S LITTLE IRONIES"

An Imaginative Woman

We may regard Southsea as being in our author's mind when he took *Solentsea* as the background for this story, but we find no clue to help us in identifying the particular house in which the Marchmonts were supposed to have lodged. Southsea is essentially a seaside resort and forms the residential quarter of Portsmouth. To the archaeologist there is little of interest attaching to the town; the castle, built by Henry VIII., stands at the southern extremity of Portsea Island. Just opposite the sea-front, and only separated from the mainland by the inlet of the English Channel, lies the Isle of Wight; doubtless this is the spot designated by our author as the "Island opposite."

If Southsea is lacking in interest, the island fully compensates for the deficiency in its high cliffs and sheltered bays, deep-wooded depressions and bare downs to the height of 700 feet above the sea.

The undercliff is a terrace of natural construction, sheltered by precipices above and behind, and offers a home to many delicate plants. On the south side of the island are the famous ravines, cut through the soft rock by the action of rivulets, mimicking the cañons of the far west where full-fed rivers rush along. The Needles, originally four in number, lie off the westernmost point; during a storm in 1764 one of the spires was undermined and fell; their chief constituent is chalk, and they are about 100 feet in height. Alum Bay is perhaps the most interesting spot to the geologist, for here the vertical disposition of the strata is very clearly defined; many fossils are to be met with, and at Brook Point there exists an extensive fossil forest.

The Son's Veto

"In a remote nook in North Wessex, forty miles from London, near the thriving town of Aldbrickham (Reading), there stood a pretty village with its church and parsonage. . . ." This introduces us to the village called *Gaymead*, and we may identify it more or less closely with Shinfield, a hamlet standing a little distance off the main road from Reading to Basingstoke, and about four miles from the former. It is certainly a pretty village; many of the

Shinfield Church *(Gaymead)*
The *Gaymead* of *The Son's Veto*, "wherein we picture the marriage of Sophy and the rector." Denys Kay-Robinson reports as oral tradition that Sulhampstead inspired *Gaymead*. The two places are not necessarily mutually exclusive and may jointly have inspired Hardy. This would account for Lea's careful phrasing: "we may identify it more or less closely with Shinfield." Windle says that "it is improbable that Mr Hardy had any special place in his mind when writing about it here, or in *Jude the Obscure* where it is again alluded to." This sounds remarkably like an answer from Hardy himself; perhaps the nature of the story suggested that too precise an identification was undesirable.

The Parish Church, Taunton *(Toneborough)*
Then, as now, a feast of architectural interest. *Toneborough* was the home of Millbourne, the hero of *For Conscience Sake*.

houses are of half-timber construction and are overhung with trees. The church is a fine example of flint-work and has a square, solid-looking brick tower with battlemented parapets and handsome string courses. It was originally built in the thirteenth century; the tower is later, perhaps sixteenth century. Inside are a number of interesting monuments, and the roof is of massive timbers, curiously strutted. This is the church wherein we picture the marriage of Sophy and the rector; and in the churchyard Sophy was supposedly laid to rest. The vicarage is near by, but it is a comparatively new building devoid of any particular interest.

A London suburb is the next background; it, however, bears no distinctive features by which we can distinguish it among two or three on the south side, though the Clapham Road would meet the description. Sophy is residing here after her widowhood, and one day she sees Sam passing along the road in the early morning with a load of vegetables for Covent Garden Market – a scene that may be witnessed any early morning in the suburbs of London. Soon after her ride beside him we are told that he takes a fruiterer's business in *Aldbrickham* – a town cast in the semblance of Reading. We can scarcely hope to pick out the actual shop after this lapse of time, and the only clue we are given regarding it is that it was the largest of its kind in the town. In our mind's eye we can see Sam standing at the door some four years later watching a funeral procession as "it passed his door and went out of the town towards the village of Gaymead."

For Conscience' Sake

From the story told by Millborne we learn that he "came up to town at one-and-twenty, from Toneborough, in Outer Wessex." *Toneborough* is our author's imaginative Taunton; the fact that it stands on the river Tone suggests to us the origin of its fictitious name, and, if we remember rightly, this tale is the first to introduce it into these chronicles. In mediaeval times the fairs – now held twice yearly – were celebrated for the sale of a woollen cloth called "Tauntons." The parish church is one of the largest and finest in the country. There are some relics of Norman work; Early English is represented in the north aisles and transepts; but the main building is Perpendicular. The castle, now used as a museum, and containing some interesting prehistoric and other antiquities, was largely rebuilt in 1496, but its original date was much earlier than this, the walls and the keep being twelfth century.

It was here that the ill-fated meeting of Millborne and Leonora was supposed to take place; but when later he

Wells *(Fountall)*
Fountall of *A Tragedy of Two Ambitions*, where old Halborough was sentenced. From Wells the action moves to West Coker (*Narrobourne*) where the "gloomy" manor is still to be seen.

wished to marry her it was to *Exonbury* he had to go in order to find her. Exeter is more or less the prototype of *Exonbury*; no particular spot is mentioned here except the house in which Leonora lived, and which cannot now be accurately determined. After a passing reference to London, and again to the Isle of Wight, the action turns to *Ivell*. In Anglo-Saxon times Yeovil was known as Evill or Ivle, and the local pronunciation to-day is Iv'll; this suffices to tell us the town figured in our author's mind as *Ivell*. Cope is represented as the curate of St. John's Church – a Perpendicular building of cruciform shape containing some fine windows of that style, and interesting brasses of the fifteenth and sixteenth centuries. Under the chancel is a thirteenth-century crypt. It is here that the Millbornes eventually come to reside, living in a "little old manor-house . . . standing a mile from Mr. Cope's town of Ivell."

A Tragedy of Two Ambitions

The action of this story is also laid in and around Yeovil. With the prologue we have little to do; the village is not mentioned by name, and is only referred to as being in a distant county. Wells, in its guise of *Fountall*, comes before us for a time, the Cathedral Close receiving frequent mention; in it we see the elder Halborough stand, "staring quizzically at the west front of the cathedral." This now old-fashioned city of Wells, lying in a hollow under the Mendip Hills, amid beautiful scenery, was one of the most important towns of Wessex in Saxon times. The 600 figures on the west front of its cathedral, most of them lifesize or larger, represent kings and queens of Saxon, Norman, and Plantagenet times, as well as many angels, prophets, and saints.

Thence the action moves to *Narrobourne*, strongly suggestive of West Coker.

On the Western Circuit

The first background to this story we find in the market-square at *Melchester* – typical of Salisbury. The fair is in full swing, and we picture Raye leaving his quiet contemplation of the cathedral – the "most homogeneous pile of mediaeval architecture in England" – and entering the turmoil in the market-place. *Melchester* has already received our consideration in previous chapters, but the house imagined to be the home of the Harmans is a fresh object to us. It was "a dignified residence of considerable size," and it gave on to the square. A building answering to the description, though not now a private residence, may be found near the north-east corner.

Our next exploration will be "the earthworks of Old

Old Sarum *(Old Melchester)*
The earthworks of *Old Melchester* (near Salisbury), mentioned in the short story *On the Western Circuit*.

Melchester," where Raye takes Anna for a walk. The associations of Old Sarum are profoundly interesting to the archaeologist; the huge mound is hollowed out in the centre like a crater, and the rim is topped by a rampart; it descends almost sheerly to a depth of one hundred feet. It was a stronghold of the early Britons. To the Romans it was known as *Sorbiodunum*. Early in the sixth century it was the seat of Cerdic, founder of the Wessex Kingdom. In the reign of Edward the Confessor it possessed a mint. In 1705 it became the seat of a bishopric, transferred thither from Sherborne. On the "Sarum Breviary," printed in Venice in 1483, was based the prayer-books of Edward VI. It was not until the thirteenth century that the new city of Salisbury sprang into existence; but the walls of the old city remained standing until early in the seventeenth century, when they were demolished. According to Ptolemy (second century) Sarum was a place of Celtic origin.

The "Great Mid-Wessex Plain" is obviously suggestive of Salisbury Plain, and it was in one of the villages lying within its boundaries that Anna was brought up – the same place in which Edith Harman had passed her early life. The actual position of this village we cannot determine, though it seems not far from Stonehenge. Unfortunately, much of the poetry of the *Great Plain* has disappeared within recent years, owing to the advent of military camps, an innovation which will appeal less to the aesthetic than to the utilitarian section of English people. This vast expanse of green downland, only occasionally broken by cultivated stretches, used to convey a sense of loneliness and remoteness from civilisation that impressed the visitor with a peculiar feeling of delight; one might wander mile after mile without meeting a single human being, and the only evidence of sentient life was to be looked for in the flocks of sheep grazing here and there, or a distant glimpse of a shepherd with his dog. But to-day that is all changed; the contours of the grassy undulations are marred by military tents or groups of temporary structures; and instead of a distant call from a shepherd, our ears are met by frequent bugle-calls.

The action turns to London, and there the marriage of our two chief characters takes place. The last we see of them is as they speed along in the train, bound for *Knollsea*, the fictitious presentment of Swanage.

To Please his Wife

Poole, the town which approximates to the *Havenpool* of the Wessex Novels, forms the background in this story. It is built on a peninsula formed by the waters of Poole

Poole Harbour *(Havenpool)*
Poole, with one of the largest natural harbours in the world, was a very important haven in the past. Many ships (with Wessex men as crew) sailed from here to the cod fisheries off Newfoundland. It is well worth visiting St James' Church, where (in *To Please His Wife*) Shadrach Joliffe offered up thanks for his narrow escape from shipwreck.

Harbour, an irregular, many-bayed inlet, and, on the other side, by Holes Bay. The harbour, with its exceedingly narrow mouth, extends nearly six miles inland, and has an average breadth of about four miles. Of the many islands which are dotted about, Branksea, or Brownsea, is the largest; on it is a castellated residence, once a castle of defence, built in the Tudor period as a safeguard for the harbour. It is a picturesque sheet of water, but by no means easy to navigate, for the ebb of the tide leaves only narrow channels, difficult to follow except to those who are really familiar with its intricacies. When viewed from the height of Nine-Barrow Down on the south, or from Lytchett Beacon on the north, the wide stretch of water, with its islands cropping up here and there, has a lake-like appearance, and has earned for itself the title of "The Dorset Lakes." At the mouth of the estuary are the Sandbanks, a low-lying stretch of loose sand which would without doubt have dissolved and filled up the channel had protecting groynes not been built to break the force of the sea. There is a double tide in the harbour; after flowing for six hours it ebbs for an hour and a half, and then flows again for the same period, thus making a second high-water, and ebbs again for the remaining three hours.

Although there are numerous barrows and British earthworks scattered about the environs of Poole, and traces exist of a Roman road leading from there to Wimborne, we possess no very early chronicles of the town. It is first mentioned historically in 1224, when "the bailiffs and good men of La Pole" were ordered to retain all ships within their port.

We are introduced to Joliffe when he is imagined as entering St. James' Church to offer up a thanksgiving for his deliverance from shipwreck. This is the parish church, erected in 1820 on the site of an ancient building. In the High Street we are also interested; it is the main thoroughfare which bisects the town and leads down to the quay. The quay is one of the most interesting parts of the town, for here forgather men of many nationalities; it also serves as a sort of club-lounge for the loafers of the town and the gossips. To the wharves come many foreign ships, laden chiefly with timber; and from here is shipped a considerable amount of the clay for which the district is famous. Close beside the quay we find the old town cellars, exhibiting the most ancient building in Poole, dating from the reign of Edward III. Looking on to the High Street is a Georgian house, now used as a hospital, and we have every reason to think this was appropriated by our author as a model for "the worthy merchant's home, one of those large substantial brick mansions

The Bridge at Lower Bockhampton
The lodging of Wat Ollamoor is shown is Lea's photograph on the left over the bridge. As is so often the case, it is extraordinary to come upon this scene today and find it quite the same as when Lea took his photograph.

frequently jammed up in old-fashioned towns."

In imagination we can picture Joanna climbing the toilsome ascent of Constitution Hill, "whence a view of the open channel could be obtained," to gaze seawards in the hope of seeing her husband's ship return. From the apex of this hill a magnificently wide view stretches before us: the harbour, broken by the many islands and inlets; the Purbeck Hills behind forming the ultimate background, with the jagged walls of Corfe Castle standing out against them; while to the eastward we can note the narrow neck of the harbour, leading into the English Channel.

The Fiddler of the Reels

When we were examining the sites and scenes in "Under the Greenwood Tree" [published in Volume 2] we recognised, close to the bridge at Lower Bockhampton, a long low house which was supposed to represent the home of Farmer Shiner. The same place comes before us now as the house at which Wat Ollamoor lodged. We hear of Car'line Aspent pausing on this bridge and becoming fascinated by the fiddler's music. At that time she was dwelling with her father, the parish clerk, who lived in the middle of the village of *Stickleford*. Tincleton has already done duty for Stickleford; there are two distinct clusters of houses here, and we are inclined to locate the clerk's house in the more western, and older, cluster, near to the farm-house which we decided to regard as the model for Venn's dairy-house in "The Return of the Native" [see Volume 2].

The action turns for a time to London, but again reverts to South Wessex. We may picture the Hipcrofts journeying to *Casterbridge* (Dorchester) by rail, and Car'line and the child setting out to walk to *Stickleford*. At "a certain half-way house, widely known as an inn," they were to await the arrival of Ned. Here, at the inn familiarised to us as *The Quiet Woman*, the mother and child find Mop Ollamoor, and when Ned comes on the scene it is to discover that Mop has disappeared and taken the little girl with him. We may picture the fancied pursuit across *Egdon*. "Outside the house, on the other side of the highway, a mass of dark heath-land rose sullenly upward to its not easily accessible interior, a ravined plateau, whereon jutted into the sky . . . the fir woods of Mistover, backed by the Yalbury coppices." This description of the scene is true to-day, excepting that the *Mistover* fir-woods have passed out of existence, burnt in some of the fires which have ravaged the heath. This section of South Wessex is very familiar to those of us who have visited the

The White Hart Inn, Dorchester
(Casterbridge)
"A large carrier's van stands in the quadrangular fore-court of the White Hart Inn, upon the sides of its spacious tilt being painted, in weather-beaten letters: 'Burthen, Carrier to Longpuddle.' These vans, so numerous hereabout, are a respectable, if somewhat lumbering, class of conveyance, much resorted to by decent travellers not overstocked with money, the better among them roughly corresponding to the old French *diligences*."

The Church at Pydelhinton
(Longpuddle)
Pydelhinton (or Puddlehinton, in the dainty vocabulary of modern bureaucrats eschewing a genuine Anglo-Saxon root) and Pydeltrenthide jointly inspired *Longpuddle*. This is the church visited by William Privett at midnight (in *The Superstitious Man's Story*). The church features also in the poem "A Sunday Morning Tragedy".

home of Eustacia Vye, and it would seem needless to describe it further here.

"A Few Crusted Characters"

If we enter Dorchester by the London Road we shall see, on our right hand, just at the commencement of the town, an inn bearing the name of the White Hart, a fine wooden specimen of that animal gracing the top of the porch. On any market day we may find the yard in front of the inn thronged with carriers' vans, all typical of the particular van mentioned in the short tales we are examining. "Burthen, Carrier to Longpuddle," is the title it bears, and in *Longpuddle* we shall recognise a strong resemblance to the villages of Pydelhinton and Pydeltrenthide, the apt naming of the fictitious place striking us at once as we explore the two long straggling villages which are practically connected to each other.

Let us follow Burthen's van as it starts from the White Hart. First come the open meadows – the *Durnover Moor* of the Wessex Novels – Grey's Bridge occurring about midway; then, taking the left-hand road, we climb Waterstone, or Climmerstone Ridge – scene of the poem entitled "The Revisitation" – by way of Slyre's Lane, which brings us to the summit by a series of rises and dips. Once at the top of the hill, the road descends into the valley of the Pydele and follows that little stream upwards, the road running parallel with the river. According to local repute, the district is one wherein a man can "neither live nor die" – which means it is too poor for him to make a living in, while the climate is too healthy to allow him to perish! It was on this road that Tony got himself into the pickle he himself describes as a "nunny-watch."

"The History of the Hardcomes" has *Budmouth-Regis* as its backgound, a place well known to us as semblable to Weymouth. "They looked at the ships in the harbour," we read, "and then went up to the Look-out," which is now called the Nothe.

In "The Superstitious Man's Story" we are interested in a matter outside the scope of mere topography. The church is not mentioned by name, but the inference points to it being the church of *Longpuddle* – which we are led to perceive as that of Pydelhinton. William Privett's midnight visit to the church porch brings before us a custom or superstition still believed in by some of the older people in the less sophisticated parts of Wessex, and the present writer has met several people who firmly believed in the custom, and who, according to their own showing, had proved its outcome to be true.

The story of "Andrey Satchel and the Parson and Clerk"

Frampton Church *(Scrimpton)*
The church at Frampton, the *Scrimpton* of the story of *Andrey Satchel and the Parson and the Clerk*, is still intact and you can see the tower where Satchel and his intended bride were locked up.

has its action at *Scrimpton*, a village nearly identical with Frampton, or Frome-town. Here, in the beautiful old church built in the fifteenth century, the wedding is imagined to have taken place. There was once a Benedictine priory at Frampton, and close to the village is the site of an ancient British settlement.

The story called "Absent-mindedness in a Parish Choir" brings back to us the novel entitled "Under the Greenwood Tree," where we find many interesting details relating to the "ecclesiastical bandsmen." The episode is supposed to have taken place in the gallery of *Longpuddle* Church, already referred to as Pydelhinton.

"The Winters and the Palmleys" takes us into *Yalbury Wood*. There used to be a curious superstition current with regard to Yellowham Wood. It was said to be the haunt of a mysterious personage known as "The Wild Man o' Yall'm," to whom was attributed the paternity of many of the "love-children" in the neighbouring villages. He was also credited with causing many unpleasant surprises to those belated souls who chanced to find themselves under the shade of the Yellowham trees after nightfall. There is an unimpeachable story of a girl who was arraigned before the local magistrates, and who, in reply to a question as to the paternity of her child, replied: "Please your Worshipfuls, 'twer' the Wild Man o' Yall'm."

To find the field of action for the "Incident in the Life of Mr. George Crookhill" we must explore the northern portion of South Wessex. "Georgy was ambling out of Melchester" and overtook a "fine-looking young farmer" near Bissett Hill. This hill is about three miles from Salisbury on the road leading through Blandford to Dorchester. At Woodyates Inn – occurring under its present-day name and easily discovered – they stopped to bait their horses; at *Trantridge* – a place akin to Pentridge – they passed the night. At East Woodyates the road intersects the old Roman Road, or Via Iceniana, which runs in a straight line to Badbury Rings. *Vindogladia*, the Roman Station, is regarded by some authorities to have been synonymous with Woodyates. The by-lane down which they are supposed to have ridden would no doubt be this same Roman Road.

We read that "the figure of Mr. Lackland was seen at the inn, and in the village street, and in the fields and lanes about Upper Longpuddle," the designation "Upper" seeming to denote Pydeltrenthide.

A Sunday Morning Tragedy

This poem depends for its background on *Pydel Vale*, a locality which figures in "Crusted Characters," where the adjoining villages of Pydelhinton and Pydeltrenthide are known to us under the joint name of *Longpuddle*. It was in the church of the former of these parishes that the banns were called, in circumstances reputed to be veracious.

THE COUNTRY OF

"A PAIR OF BLUE EYES"

In order to discover the land- and sea-scapes from which the theatre of this story was drawn, we shall have to go to the most westerly portion of that great area familiar to us as Wessex. This particular tract concerns us only in this one book, and practically the whole of it is contained within a short radius of the quaint sea-washed town of Boscastle. There are a few other scenes, it is true – in London, at Plymouth, and in spots still more remote; – but those touched with local characterisation are within the area named.

Lest my readers should be disappointed later, it may be as well to state frankly at the outset that we shall have somewhat to readjust several of the features we are intent on discovering ere we can make them coincide with the artificial representations given us in the story. This was one of our author's earliest books, written forty or so years ago, and the alterations worked by time on the real spots, together with, perhaps, to a still greater extent the modifications due at the outset to imaginative treatment, account for any inaccuracy apparent in the scenes pictured when regarded as delineations of the actual ones we see to-day. But this applies only to certain architectural features and their positions; the natural configurations are vividly realistic.

The tale has a unique interest in being the only one of the series in which the heroine is positively known to have been suggested by a real person. Before commencing our researches we may glance for a moment at the general topography of the district.

The county of Cornwall possesses, as is well known, an individuality difficult to describe, but nevertheless very distinct. Within its boundaries is included a great dissimilarity of scenery. We have the romantic moorlands, broken up with the outcropping of gaunt jagged rocks, bare, desolate; the seventy miles between Launceston and Mount's Bay has been described as "the dreariest strip of earth traversed by any English high road." Then we have the long valleys, flanked by grassy downs, many of them deep and narrow and densely wooded, through which the little rivers dance and jump from rock to rock and seldom follow a straight line for many yards together. On the coast

The Castle, Launceston *(St Launce's)*
Lea's photograph shows the most noteworthy feature of the town.

Launceston *(St Launce's)*
The nearest station to Launceston, today, is Bodmin Parkway. Readers are advised to explore from Boscastle by car. *Camelton* (Camelford) station still exists, but there is no railway line.

we find three very distinct types of scenery: the dark, rugged slate cliffs; the serpentine rock with its marvellous colouring; and the majestic, adamantine granite. This last is particularly seen in the neighbourhood of Land's End; it crops out again in the Scilly Isles, said traditionally to have been once joined to the mainland, the submerged portion forming the ancient land called Lyonesse, and imagined to have contained 140 parish churches. Owing to the prevailing dampness and the heavy dews, the lower levels of the county displayed no extraordinary aridness in the late abnormally dry summer of 1911; the grass remained green, and growth appeared to be of the average, if not greater. On the west coast, as late as the end of October, many wild flowers might have been seen still in lusty bloom: gorse, heather, violets, blackberry blossom, and many others. Fuchsias here grow into trees, many of them blossoming high above the roofs of the cottages, while in the deep sheltered valleys the vegetation is luxuriant and extremely varied.

To return to that portion of the county with which we are most intimately concerned. At the time when the story commences the nearest railway station to *Endelstow* was *St. Launce's* – a name which easily suggests Launceston to the least discerning reader. But later a station was opened at *Camelton* – an obvious representation of Camelford. To-day there is another station still nearer, viz. Otterham. But those who propose to make an examination of the places to be presently described would find Boscastle the most convenient centre from which to explore. If, however, we prefer to follow Stephen Smith as he approaches *Endelstow* vicarage from *St. Launce's*, we shall be at once struck with the realistic description of the country from Launceston to the north coast near Boscastle. To the present writer the following details presented themselves with an almost uncanny similitude: "Scarcely a solitary house or man had been visible along the whole dreary distance of open country. . . . The only lights apparent on earth were some spots of dull red, glowing here and there upon the distant hills . . . smouldering fires for the consumption of peat and gorse-roots."

If we inquire our way and follow the lanes indicated, we shall be able to verify the hilly character given to this district: "They climbed a hill, then another piled on the summit of the first . . . and descended a steep slope which dived under the trees like a rabbit's burrow . . . and the chimneys and gables of the vicarage became darkly visible".

There is ground for supposing that in describing this vicarage the writer had largely in his mind the rectory of

The Path to St Juliot Rectory
Endelstow, or St Juliot Rectory, remains almost as described by Hardy, though, like so many original vicarages, it is now privately owned.

St. Juliot. It is a much pleasanter journey thither than by the above route to take the footpath which leads us through the Vallency valley from Boscastle. In the autumn, when the trees are changing colour, the scenery is particularly enchanting. The valley is a deep one and very narrow; close beside us on our right hand the little river takes its serpentine course, babbling fretfully over the rocks which form its bed; sometimes there are still, quiet pools in which speckled trout may be discovered lurking close beside the stones; in other spots it hurls itself down miniature cascades; then for a time it flows in placid contentment. The hill on our right hand is clothed with dwarf trees, chiefly oaks, all leaning eastward with one accord, away from the prevailing winds, which have razed off their tops to a dead level, as though they had been trimmed by a pair of giant shears. The branches, sometimes to the topmost twigs, are shrouded in feathery grey lichen, testifying to the damp atmosphere which is so prevalent here. On our left hand the mountain is more broken, craggy rocks spring out here and there, and the intervening ground is covered with furze, rough grass, bracken, and stunted bushes.

As the path mounts gradually higher the stream gurgles some feet below us, and we soon catch a glimpse of the rectory of St. Juliot on our left hand, standing amidst a thick clump of trees, and a couple of fields away from the path. No actual details are given us in the narrative of the house itself, but from its position, apart from other reasons, we feel we are not very wide of the mark in claiming it as the model for *Endelstow Vicarage*.

From this observation point we can see the tower of the church a little distance ahead, and over the valley to the right we catch the pinnacled tower of another church – that of Lesnewth – of which more anon.

The church before us is the one we have cause to accept as the prototype of *West Endelstow*, a background to many important scenes. It is dedicated to St. Julietta, a martyr, respecting whom very little is known. In the churchyard is an ancient cross, once intended doubtless to fix a preaching-place; on the disc which surmounts the shaft is a boldly cut Maltese cross, or perhaps we should say a *patée*. The church is of the Perpendicular order of architecture, a type most usual throughout Cornwall. It is solidly built of granite-ashlar, and, like most Cornish churches, possesses very little ornamentation. It was restored in 1872, and a tablet of Sicilian marble on a ground of Carnsew granite has been recently erected in the north aisle to record the fact that the late Mrs. Thomas Hardy before her marriage laid the foundation-stone of

St Juliot Church *(Endelstow)*
The church as it appeared before the restoration in 1872. Hardy was personally involved in the restoration project and it was thus that he met Emma Lavinia Gifford, who became his wife in 1874 There is a considerable amount of autobiography in *A Pair of Blue Eyes.*

the new portions, and conducted the music of the church while living at the rectory here with her sister and brother-in-law. Apart from this circumstantial evidence it has been generally understood for a long time that the personal appearance and even the character of Elfride were studied in some particulars from this lady as she showed herself in youth; though the other personages and the dramatic incidents of the story are quite fictitious.

But although we choose to recognise this as the church we are in search of, its position must not be accepted. From the description given in the story we must imagine it as standing on the other side of the rectory, nearer to the sea, and close to the summit of the hill. There is a point of view below us in the valley where the church appears to stand more nearly to its supposed position; but even then we cannot bring it into proper focus with the rectory. We read of its environment: "Not a tree could exist up there: nothing but the monotonous grey-green grass" – a description which fixes it indubitably at the top of the hill in the full stroke of the west wind, and reveals to us that something of the situation has been borrowed from the site of Forrabury Church a couple of miles off. However, a stone stile gives access to the churchyard of St. Juliot, just as in our story. On one of the tombs may be seen this quaintly worded inscription:

> Her Raging disease Mock'd the powers of Medicine, and Snatch'd with Resistless Impetuosity an Indulgent Parent from her growing Offsprings.

Trebarwith Strand, which lies some five miles to the south of Boscastle, is by its very name suggestive of the *Barwith Strand* of the story, but there is no detailed description allotted to it. It was merely the object of an excursion, and for other than that has no particular claim to notice here. "Barwith Strand . . . was duly visited. They then swept round by innumerable lanes, in which not twenty consecutive yards were either straight or level. . . ." This description of the roads – or rather lanes – of the locality is strongly borne out by personal experience. In passing along one of the old Roman roads the traveller very often becomes wearied with the monotonous straightness of its construction; but nothing can exceed the vexatious nature of these twisting Cornish lanes which enlarge the distance from place to place amazingly. They are beautiful, it is true, very beautiful; often overhung with trees whose topmost branches intertwine, and through which the sunlight pierces its way with difficulty, tracing strange Oriental patterns on the road; sometimes

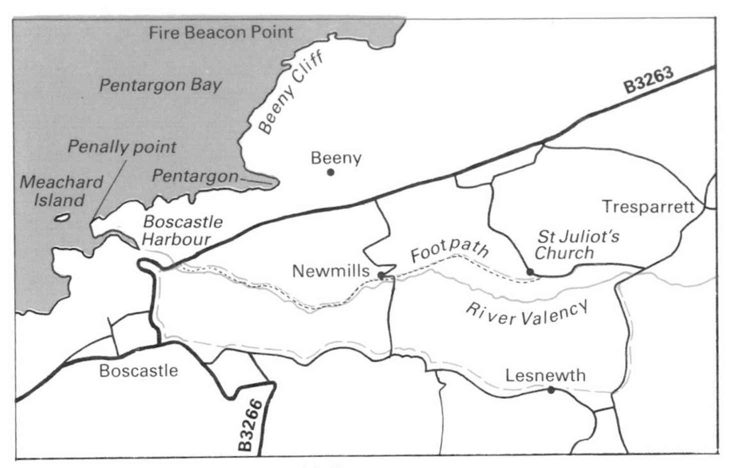

A Walk Through the Valency Valley

walled in with high banks covered with flowers, or loose-jointed stone walls in whose interstices ferns and sedums flourish; but nevertheless they are better designed for an inconsequent stroll than for the speedy attainment of any definite goal.

It was by way of these twisting lanes that Stephen and Elfride were supposed to have reached *Endelstow House* – the seat of Lord Luxellian. Whether such a house ever existed in the locality is doubtful: certainly there is no such place at the present time; though there is one answering to the description some twenty miles south of this parish. Anyhow, its position in the story may be gauged as being somewhere between *East* and *West Endelstow* villages.

The next scene we shall inquire into is one in which the cliffs formed the background. Stephen and Elfride had a memorable expedition to "the cliffs beyond Targan Bay." The direction they took, combined with the fact that the cliff is later described as being the second highest in the vicinity, leads us to infer that the reference is to the precipitous verge known locally as "Strangles," a name the origin of which is not clear. Nearly the whole of the coastline of this district is wild in the extreme; jagged black rocks rise sheerly from the sea, forming precipitous walls, cruel and forbidding in appearance, and dangerous to walk upon. By inquiring our way to Strangles Cliff we shall in due course light upon a scene which seems vividly familiar to those of us who have read "A Pair of Blue Eyes." Beneath us is "the everlasting stretch of ocean." There are the "detached rocks," the "white screaming gulls," the "toothed and zig-zag line of storm-torn heights." With a westerly or north-westerly wind urging them onwards, the waves hurl themselves against the craggy cliff-face with terrific force, and a noise as of thunder which is deafening to listen to; the wind seems to clutch at the clumps of heather and gorse and rough grass as though the tentacles of some giant octopus were grasping to wrench them from the soil. The seabirds wheel and dart and scream; and far overhead may be seen the lordly peregrine falcon – now becoming so rare in our islands – sailing on outstretched pinions, or darting forward with his marvellously rapid flight, or stooping to some quarry on the earth far below him. The scene is bright and gay when the sun is shining, but when the sky is overcast with clouds a subtle sullenness seems to settle down on sea and land, and hang like an oppressive weight over all nature.

Later on in the story we visit the same spot with Elfride and Knight, and on that occasion our author gives this cliff

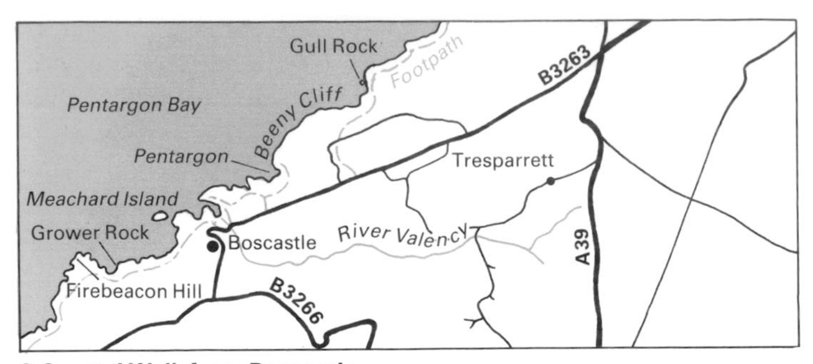

A Coastal Walk from Boscastle

the name of *Windy Beak* – a title which was probably suggested to him by Cam Beak, a cliff jutting out into the sea farther to the north.

Another sea-picture comes before our eyes when we read of Knight and Elfride visiting *Targan Bay* on their way to the scene of the adventure which so nearly proved disastrous. There can be very little doubt in our minds that *Targan Bay* was drawn from Pentargan, a narrow inlet scarcely deserving the name of bay, which lies a short two miles from Boscastle northwards. The description given us of the journey thither from *Endelstow* vicarage is a true facsimile of what we see to-day. There are still the "neutral green hills," the "chocolate-toned rocks" on both sides of the steep roads. We will follow in the footsteps of Elfride when, starting from the vicarage, she "ascended and passed over a hill" until she came to a "small stream. . . . It was smaller than that in her own valley. . . . Bushes lined the slopes of its shallow trough; but at the bottom, where the water ran, was a soft green carpet, in a strip two or three yards wide." We may take precisely the same track and follow the stream until we reach the ledge of rock over which it precipitates itself on to the rocks deep below. It was at this spot that they paused – Knight having now joined her – and gazed out to sea, noting the "nebulous haze, stretching like gauze" over it. This haze is one of the predominant characteristics of the western coasts; for we note the same peculiarity on the west coast of Wales and of Ireland.

If we visit this spot on a day when Nature is morose in mood, the "nebulous haze" will appear as a heavy, inky pall brooding over everything. The cliffs and rocks are of a dingy slate-colour; slate-coloured is the sea and the sky and the pebbles on the strand; even the grass looks less green than murky.

Leaving the bay with its miniature beach, and the flanking walls tunnelled with caves, we will turn our attention to the steep cliff farther on, which is known to readers as "the cliff without a name" (a statement afterwards qualified and explained in the preface to the later editions). To the local resident this cliff passes by the name of Beeny, or Beeny High Cliff. Granting our surmise as to the identify of *Targan Bay* to have been correct, then this unchristened cliff falls into position as Beeny in disguise. It is a dangerous spot, as are most of the cliffs on this wild, wind-wrecked coast, and has been the scene of more than one tragedy. Its colour of slate-black, or more strictly dark purple, adds to its forbidding appearance, only a few thin streaks of white marble breaking in a slight degree its sombre face. This cliff and one a little beyond

Boscastle Harbour *(Castle Boterel)*
"The place is pre-eminently (for one person at least) the region of dream and mystery. The ghostly birds, the pall-like sea, the frothy wind, the eternal soliloquy of the waters, the bloom of dark purple cast, that seems to exhale from the shoreward precipices, in themselves lend to the scene an atmosphere like the twilight of a night vision."

share the local reputation of being the highest in Cornwall, controversy on the subject of its actual, measurable height often leading to staunch declarations and spirited retorts. "Haggard cliffs," says our author, "of every ugly altitude, are as common as sea-fowl along the line of coast between Exmoor and Land's End; but this out-flanked and encompassed specimen was the ugliest of them all" – a contention which few who know the coast will be prepared to deny.

Of *Castle Boterel* we hear several times in the course of the narrative. Its identity with Boscastle may be readily guessed at, although of course it was the Boscastle of forty or more years ago which our author looked on as his model. To-day it is a very favourite resort with tourists, who become familiar with its likeness in many of the carriages on the South-Western Railway. Once there was a Norman mansion standing here, and it was known as Bottreaux Castle (though an old resident gives it as Boterel), but only its site is visible as a grass-covered mound a short distance from the village up the Jordan Valley. The harbour is cunningly contrived: Nature has sheltered it to some extent by the prominent headland called Penally Point; and human ingenuity has fashioned rough stone piers to complete the work. It is a tortuous passage, and ships have to be warped up to the landing-stage. Through the headland just referred to there is a blow-hole, and at a certain level of the tide the water spurts through this tunnel in a dense spray or jet, as though forced by some mechanical agency. Curious, eerie noises proceed from the opening. Just off Penally Point is a tiny rock-island, called Meachard Island, once doubtless joined to the mainland, a favourite breeding-place of many gulls. There is a curious tradition connected with the parish church of St. Symphorian, Forrabury, which stands high on Willapark Point, in full view of the Atlantic. The tower is without bells, and a ballad by the Cornish poet, Robert Stephen Hawker, tells of a ship bearing bells hither being wrecked outside the harbour, and that the sunk bells may be heard tolling beneath the waves.

The port and town itself has lost some of its former picturesqueness by the demolition of many of the older cottages and the erection of new villas of prosaic architectural form. The roofs are all of slate – in strong contrast to the thatch we generally find in the central and northern portions of Wessex – but that is only to be expected, since the famous slate quarries of Delabole are so close at hand. Luckily, however much of this slate is of a pale grey colour, and it "weathers" to a shade by no means

The White Hart, Launceston
(The Falcon, St Launce's)
The model for *The Falcon* remains well worth a visit.

disagreeable to the eyes.

There are several backgrounds in this book which we cannot discover. These we shall therefore regard as being either entirely fictitious, imported from elsewhere, or as having disappeared during the time which has elapsed since the book was written. *Endelstow House* aforesaid, its lodge, the cottage inhabited by Stephen's father, and other features are among these. The "ancient manor-house" which is supposed to have stood close to the vicarage was very probably drawn from an old house called Tregrylls, now entirely demolished, but which used to stand on the other side of the Vallency Valley.

With Plymouth (figuring under its own name) we have little to do. We read of Stephen spending an hour there whilst waiting for his train to London, and walking on the Hoe, whence can be seen "the wide Sound, the breakwater, the lighthouse on far-off Eddystone." Thither, too, we may follow Elfride a fortnight later, when she goes to join him there and be married secretly. We may picture her leaving the valley of her home and mounting to an open tableland from whence she had a view of the sea. Once again our interest is directed to Plymouth, on the occasion of the supposed journey from London by steamer. We see the travellers as they pass in succession, the Nore, the South Foreland, Dover, Beachy Head, Southampton, Portland Bill, the Race, the Chesil Beach, West Bay, Start Point, Bolt Head, Forward Point, Berry Head, Prawle – till finally Plymouth is reached.

St. Launce's is a town often receiving mention. At the time the story opens it was the nearest railway station to *Endelstow*. To it rode Elfride on her way to Plymouth, mentioned just above. "Presently the quaint gables and jumbled roofs of St. Launce's were spread beneath her, and going down the hill she entered the courtyard of the Falcon." Launceston is surprisingly full of interest to the archaeologist and the antiquarian. Of its history prior to the Conquest little is known, but the finding of Roman coins in the vicinity is not without suggestion, and we may infer it possessed a history anterior to that of the Norman invasion. At one time the town was walled, and could show three gateways, only one of which remains standing to-day. The rooms above this archway are used as a museum and contain many exceedingly interesting antiquities. Probably the "White Hart Hotel" served our author as original for the *Falcon*. It has a fine Norman doorway, once pertaining to the Abbey which stood close to St. Thomas's Church, but of which nothing remains save the ruins. No one can visit Launceston without being struck by the ornate character of the parish church of St.

Lesnewth Church *(East Endelstow Church)*

Mary Magdalene, an early Tudor erection. The elaborate carving on the outer walls is teeming with interesting designs, but unfortunately its aspect is much marred by an incongruous figure in pink terra-cotta which stands in a niche over the south porch. The tower, which is at least a century older than the church, was originally detached from it, but is now joined by a building used as a vestry, but once a shop.

The most noteworthy feature of the town is undoubtedly the Castle, which stands on an eminence, its circular keep overtopping the town beneath. From the apex of the keep extends a marvellous view on all sides, proving the importance which must have at one time attached to the ancient fortress.

For a little while the action is diverted to London, whither it is needless for us to track the characters. *Bede's Inn* (probably Clement's Inn), Kensington, Hyde Park, the Drive and the Row, require no time to be spent in describing them. Killarney, as well as the foreign towns mentioned, we shall leave discreetly alone.

The house in which Mrs. Swancourt was supposed to reside was called *The Crags*, but we can find no trace of it to-day. Mention is made of a rock in the valley which had the contour of a man's face. There are many craggy rocks in the Vallency Valley, but we fail to recognise this particular one, though such contours do occur hereabout, and mature acquaintance with our author's methods leads us to assume that such a rock did actually exist there at the time the book was written; but weather-action will soon alter such characteristics or entirely efface them in a comparatively short time. Mrs. Jethway's cottage stands by the brook in the Vallency Valley, about half-way between *Endelstow Vicarage* and *Castle Boterel*, and has been repaired and brightened up since the time of the story.

Of all the churches in the vicinity perhaps that of Lesnewth may be taken as most nearly approximating to the one called *East Endelstow*: we have already seen its pinnacled tower from the valley road.

Our survey is now almost ended. The penultimate background is at *Camelton* railway station – distinctly suggestive of Camelford. Here we read of Knight and Stephen arriving one night in company with the "sombre van" which had travelled down on the same train as themselves. We may track them walking "in the darkness up the miles of road from Camelton to Endelstow." They paused for shelter from the rain at the blacksmith's shop – a place which is found by inquiry from local inhabitants to have been closed "this many years." It was here they first

The Ship *(The Welcome Home)*
Lea claims that this is based on The Ship at Boscastle. In fact the building still exists today, albeit a private house. It can be found in Vallency Road, a cobbled street just off the main road in Boscastle.

learnt of Elfride's marriage to Lord Luxellian and were shown the coffin-plate. Subsequently they entered an inn called the *Welcome Home* to obtain further particulars. Of this inn we can discover no sure trace; it partially recalls "The Ship" at Boscastle.

We may imagine them when on the following day they walk "up the familiar valley (Vallency Valley) to East Endelstow church" to attend the funeral. And after it is over we picture them retracing their steps "down the grey still valley to Castle Boterel."

Melbury House *(King's Hintock Court)*
Still to be seen in its original majesty, Melbury House was once the seat of the Earl of Ilchester and Hardy caused some offence to the family by writing this story.

THE COUNTRY OF "A GROUP OF NOBLE DAMES"

Dame the First

The First Countess of Wessex

The first description which we have to examine is *King's Hintock Court* – "one of the most imposing of the mansions that overlook our beautiful Blackmoor or Blakemoor Vale." This was probably drawn from Melbury House, near Evershot, a mansion partly of Elizabethan design, standing in a park containing several lakes and some fine timber, including a magnificent double avenue of sycamores.

In *Falls-Park* we recognise a likeness to Mells, the description of the mansion and its environs enabling us to identify it with some degree of certainty. "Its classic front, of the period of the second Charles . . . the densely-timbered Park . . ." strikes the beholder with a certain sense of familiarity when he sees Mells before him. The theatre of the story is continually changing as we follow the fortunes of "Mistress Betty." We picture Squire Dornell leaving Mells, and riding "along the dead level which stretches between the hills skirting Falls-Park and those bounding the town of Ivell (assumed to be Yeovil)," as he makes his way to *King's Hintock Court*. Certain friends come to him here, amongst them "the doctor from Evershead (Evershot) . . . Baxby of Sherton Castle (Sherborne)." *Evershead* is the village to which Tupcombe rides to learn news of Betty, and we see him in imagination halting at the *Sow-and-Acorn* – obviously sketched from the present "Acorn Inn".

Of the position of the house fictitiously called *Elm-Cranlynch* we have no clue, though we may not be altogether wide of the mark in finding a connection between it and Montacute, an Elizabethan mansion standing in a picturesque village four miles west of Yeovil, near the "view tower" which occupies the site of one of William the Conqueror's strongholds.

We read of the Squire's ride to Bristol, and of Betty's subsequent elopement. We will follow her when, in company with Phelipson, she leaves the Court "by an obscure gate to the east," and in due time enters "the solitary length of the old Roman road now called Long Ash

Mells *(Falls Park)*
Falls Park was modelled on Mells, a mansion which historically was owned by the Horner family. (According to Windle the Little Jack Horner of the nursery rhyme had belonged to the family. His plum arrived in the shape of property acquired at the time of the dissolution of the monasteries.)

Horton Inn *(Lornton Inn)*
It was here that Barbara Grebe met Edmond Willowes on the night of their elopement and where later she encountered Lord Uplandtowers. In the story Hardy refers to it as "the rendez-vous of many a daring poacher for operations in the adjoining forest." It still stands today, enlarged and modernised.

Farrs *(Yewsholt Lodge)*
One and a half miles west of Wimborne we find Farrs, the location of *Yewsholt Lodge*. It has been restored to its original eighteenth-century beauty.

Lane" – a road explored in the short story entitled "Interlopers at the Knap" [see Volume 2]. It may be mentioned in passing that the wretchedly deficient nomenclature of the new ordnance maps is shown by the fact that, though this lane is named in the old copies, the recently issued ones leave it undesignated. They are supposed to have halted at a "mean roadside inn." Stagg's Folly, Prince's Place, or Southfield Hill – lonely houses on that highway – more or less demolished since the date of the story – might have indicated the locality of the inn.

Dame the Second

Barbara of the House of Grebe

This grim tale opens at a point on the "turnpike road connecting Havenpool (Poole) and Warborne (Wimborne) with the city of Melchester (Salisbury)." In *Knollingwood Hall* we trace a resemblance to the mansion in St. Giles Park, about two miles south of Cranborne. This fine example of battlemented architecture dates from the sixteenth century and encloses a quadrangular court; but much of the original building has been renovated or rebuilt. It is famous as the birthplace of Anthony Cooper, afterwards Baron Ashley. In the grounds is a grotto, constructed principally of Indian shells, which is said to have cost £10,000. It is stated that the first cabbage grown in England was cultivated in the garden of St. Giles.

Chene Manor is more or less portrayed from Canford Manor, and was the supposititious residence of Sir John and Lady Grebe. The mansion was rebuilt during the last century, but some of the older portions remain, including "John of Gaunt's Kitchen," with its huge fireplace and many ancient cooking vessels.

Lornton Inn is described as "the rendezvous of many a daring poacher for operations in the adjoining forest." Horton Inn, which is its prototype, stands at the cross-roads about four miles from Wimborne, and was at one time a noted posting-house where the stage-coaches proceeding from London to Exeter were accustomed to change horses.

The *Yewsholt Lodge* of the story – "a small place on the plan of a large one" – was the house pictured as the scene of Barbara's ghastly experience after her marriage, and if we would find the model that served our author we must go to the little hamlet of Farrs, about a mile and a half to the west of Wimborne, where such a secluded house, with a small gallery round the hall, is still standing.

Wilton House, Near Salisbury
"A classical mansion . . . not a hundred miles from the city of Melchester." In a note to Lea, dated 26 September, 1911, Hardy confirms that the "classical mansion" of *The Marchioness of Stonehenge* is Wilton.

Broadlands *(Deansleigh Park)*
On the same postcard from Hardy to Lea (see left), Hardy asked for Lea's reassurance about the real models for *Deansleigh Park* and *Fernell Hall*, claiming that "it will save the trouble of reading the stories through if you can tell me." Lea was able to confirm *Deansleigh Park* as Broadlands (which later became the seat of the Mountbattens) and *Fernell Hall* as Embley House, which at one time was the home of Florence Nightingale and is now a school.

Dame the Third

The Marchioness of Stonehenge

There is very little in this story for the topographer to unravel. The Marchioness "lived in a classical mansion . . . not a hundred miles from the city of Melchester" (we read), and we recognise it as a fictitious presentment of Wilton House, near Salisbury. This historic mansion teems with interest. According to tradition, Shakespeare is supposed to have played here with his company before James I.; the picture galleries, containing a superb collection of old masters, and including some fine examples of Holbein, Vandyke, etc., are too well known to need mention; many marble statues adorn the entrance hall and cloisters. The older portion of the house is Italian sixteenth-century work. Wilton was a seat of the West Saxon kings, and was at one time a town of considerable prosperity.

Dame the Fourth

Lady Mottisfont

The first scene to which we are spirited in this romance is the interior of Winchester Cathedral, familiar to Hardy readers as *Wintoncester*, one of the most fascinating of all the towns which figure in the Wessex Novels, its charm being enhanced by its situation in a deep hollow surrounded by chalky downlands. The town has already come before us in our explorations into the country of "Tess of the d'Urbervilles," but our interest at the present juncture is confined to the Cathedral.

It holds the record of being the longest cathedral in England – about 556 feet from end to end. The exterior suffers much as a whole from lacking all but the base of the central tower, which is unobtrusive and scarcely to be marked from any great distance. Our author's description is so realistic that a vivid impression remains in the reader's mind of the spot whereon Sir Ashley Mottisfont is supposed to ask Philippa to marry him.

We have nothing further to do with the town in the story, but a ramble through Winton – to give it its ancient name – must prove interesting. According to tradition, it was first founded ninety-nine years before the building of Rome. Research has revealed that the Itchen Valley was once the home of Celtic peoples; and the fact that six Roman roads diverge from here goes to show its importance in Romano-British times. Its historical greatness commences perhaps at the date when it was the capital of Wessex; and when the kings of Wessex became the kings

Longleat House
The model for "Maria Heymere's faire maner-place" in *The Lady Icenway*. Icenway House itself is identified by Lea as being based on Marwell Hall (over page).

Embley House *(Fernell Hall)*

of England Winton was as much the capital of the country as London. Winton, too, must be ever associated in the mind with King Arthur and his knights.

Deansleigh Park, the home of Sir Ashley Mottisfont, may be sought for near Romsey, and we can safely regard Broadlands as the pattern present in our author's mind. This house stands just outside the town and can be seen from the bridge which we cross on entering the town from Salisbury. In *Fernell Hall* we find a resemblance to Embley House, famous from its association with Florence Nightingale. It stands about two miles west of Romsey on the Salisbury road. For a time the action turns to Bath, but it soon reverts to *Deansleigh Park* and the country around that spot.

Dame the Fifth

The Lady Icenway

"In 'a faire maner-place' . . . in one o' the greenest bits of woodland between Bristol and the city of Exonbury (Exeter)," lived Maria Heymere and her uncle. We find its counterpart in Longleat House, a magnificent mansion standing in its ancient deer park amid surrounding woods and forests which would be hard to equal in their display of timber and picturesque scenery. The house is distant five miles from the market-town of Warminster, which separated Salisbury Plain from the woods and meadowlands. Warminster is mentioned in Domesday Book as a royal manor whose tenant was bound to provide a night's lodging for the king and his retinue – a mandate which was enforced by George III when he visited Longleat. Longleat House is one of the largest, as also one of the most beautiful, in the country of Wilts, and dates from the sixteenth century. The word "leat" means a conduit, and refers in the present instance to the long narrow mere which crosses the park from north to south; formerly it conveyed water to the mill once attached to the priory which was founded at Horningham in the thirteenth century. The house was built by Sir John Thynne, but the name of its designer appears to be unknown. Its style is distinctly Italian; Doric, Ionic, and Corinthian orders being represented.

The only other place we have mention of is the house in which Maria is supposed to have lived after her marriage to Lord Icenway, and where Anderling followed her and subsequently died. For this we must travel "beyond Wintoncester, quite at t'other end of Wessex," until we reach Marwell Hall, famous as holding the coffer historically associated with "The Mistletoe Bough".

Marwell Hall *(Icenway House)*

The Gateway, Stalbridge Park
(Stapleford Park)
The gateway to the *Stapleford Park* of *Squire Petrick's Lady* survives.

Dame the Sixth

Squire Petrick's Lady

We are told at the outset that the "splendid old mansion" in *Stapleford* is now pulled down. *Stapleford* is typical of Stalbridge, and as in the tale nothing now remains of the real Stalbridge House; the park wall, and the gateway which opens into it, the gateposts adorned with a lion's head and trunk, are all that survive as indication of its former grandeur. The little town shows us a remarkably fine example of a market-cross; it is covered with elaborate carvings, is thirty feet in height, and dates probably from some time in the fourteenth century. The destruction of the house prevents our following the events within it.

Dame the Seventh

Anna, Lady Baxby

This romance carries us a long way back in history, to the time of the Great Rebellion, when so many castles now in ruins were at the height of their prosperity. *Sherton Castle*, where almost the entire action takes place, is an instance in point, since only a few walls, mantled in ivy and overrun with vagrant greenery, remain to us to-day as evidence of the majestic building which once stood there. Sherborne, fictitiously presented as *Sherton Abbas*, has no indications of either Roman or British settlement, and its history probably dates only from after the Saxon conquest in the seventh century. Here, in the year 705, St. Aldhelm fixed his bishop's stool for the new diocese of Western Wessex. Ethelbert, king of Wessex, was buried here in 866; and for a time the town figured as the actual capital of Wessex.

The castle was built by Bishop Roger of Caen, and was once described by Henry of Huntingdon as being scarcely inferior to that of Devizes, "than which there was none greater within the confines of England." It passed through many vicissitudes. Owing to its strength, Stephen wrested it by force from Bishop Roger; and later Elizabeth gave it to Sir Walter Raleigh, though only on a leasehold tenure.

In 1905 a pageant was invented and arranged in commemoration of the twelve hundredth anniversary of the town, the bishopric, and the school. This was held in the grounds of the castle, and set the fashion for the successive pageants which have since taken place in other towns.

The story before us is based on historical facts, and we are told that "the Parliament forces sat down before

Sherborne Castle *(Sherton Castle)*
"In the time of the great Civil War . . . the Parliament forces sat down before Sherton Castle."

Sherton Castle with over seven thousand foot and four pieces of cannon." The besiegers were under the command of Lady Baxby's brother – an obvious pseudonym for Digby – and out of consideration for her he postponed hostilities for a time; but while he still hesitated to commence an attack Lord Baxby arrived with reinforcements, before whom he retreated "to a hill near Ivell (Yeovil), four or five miles off." For all this there is much foundation in local chronicles.

Sherborne possesses many objects of interest to the archaeologist and the antiquarian. From 998 to 1539 it was the seat of a Benedictine Monastery, in which latter year its Abbey was dissolved. It was never a town protected by an enclosing wall, but depended on the fortified bishop's palace and its natural marshy environs for safety from invasion. King Alfred is supposed to have passed the greater portion of his boyhood here, and also to have received his education in this town. The handsome conduit standing in the old market-place – a spot depicted in "The Woodlanders" – dates from the sixteenth century; its building is attributed to Abbot Mere; it stood originally inside the Cloister Court of the Abbey Church, but was later moved to its present position.

The Abbey Church exhibits some Norman work; also a portion of outside wall generally attributed to a pre-Norman period; Early English and Perpendicular styles are also represented. Sherborne School and the Almshouse well repay careful inspection, though neither occur as features in the Wessex Novels.

Dame the Eighth

The Lady Penelope

The position of the house from which our author drew the first setting for this story is accurately described at the commencement of the narrative. "In going out of Casterbridge (Dorchester) by the low-lying road which eventually conducts to the town of Ivell (Yeovil), you see on the right hand an ivied manor house, flanked by battlemented towers, and more than usually distinguished by the size of its many mullioned windows." The house is conspicuously prominent from the Great Western Railway line soon after the train emerges from Poundbury tunnel; it is called Wolfeton House and stands a little distance back from the high road; directly behind it is the village of Charminster, in the parish church of which is the tomb marking the spot where the Lady Penelope and her last husband are supposed to have been buried. Whether this be so or not, her marriage with her three suitors successively is a fairly

The Gate-house, Wolfeton House
This is the model for "an ivied manor house, flanked by battlemented towers, and more than usually distinguished by the size of its many mullioned windows." (*The Lady Penelope*). The house is still there today, complete with towers and mullioned windows.

well known tradition.

Wolfeton House was rebuilt by one of the Trenchards during the reign of Henry VII., but certain portions exhibit unmistakable signs of having belonged to a period much earlier. The gate-house, with a round tower on each side, is probably of Norman origin. The interior of the house shows us some interesting and handsome carving.

A legend connects the dining-room with "the ghost of Lady Trenchard," which is supposed to have appeared previous to her death, the result of suicide.

THE COUNTRY OF "A LAODICEAN"

The townlet of Dunster provides us with a facsimile of the background against which most of the action in this story takes place; but we must not attempt so close a comparison of the actual with the factitious as we have achieved in some other instances. That Dunster Castle served in a great measure as the model for *Stancy Castle* we may be certain; but if we approach it to-day, our minds filled with a picture of the building as it appeared to George Somerset, we shall feel constrained to admit that certain features and details must have been supplied by our author, either from imagination or from the reminiscences of other architectural piles.

The name Dunster prepares us to some extent for the situation of the castle. Tor means tower; dun means hill; and hence we are not surprised to find an almost precipitous hill, clothed with grand old trees, from which the richly coloured stone towers and parapets rise against the skyline. The history of the castle carries us a long way back in time. When Edward the Confessor was king, Dunster Castle was held by Aluric, but William the Conqueror made it over to William de Mohun. During the Parliamentary wars its politics changed rapidly: first it declared for the Parliament, afterwards for King Charles; then it was besieged for several months by Cromwell's forces, to whom it finally surrendered. In 1376 it was purchased by the ancestors of the present owner.

As we enter from the north the little town of Dunster – called *Markton* in the novel – the castle occupies a very commanding position, towering above the houses. The main street is exceptionally wide, and near its centre stands the old Yarn Market, an octagonal wooden building with wide overhanging eaves and eight little dormer-windows. It is crowned by a lantern, from which rises a weather-vane with the initials G. L., and bearing the date of 1647. On the left-hand side is a remarkably fine old inn – the "Luttrell Arms" – containing many details of archaeological interest. In all probability our author's conception of the "Lord Quantock Arms" was derived from this. There is an atmosphere of mediaevalism pervading the little town; no insidious modern innovations have been allowed to creep in; and we seem to be

Dunster *(Markton)*
The castle which occupies a commanding position over the village. C. J. P. Beatty has argued that Corfe Castle in Dorset was as much a model for *Stancy Castle* as Dunster Castle.
Stancy Castle is described by Hardy as "not exceptionally large, but it had all the characteristics of its most important fellows. Irregular, dilapidated, and muffled in creepers as a great portion of it was, some part – a comparatively modern wing – was inhabited, for a light or two steadily gleamed from some upper windows; in others a reflection of the moon denoted that unbroken glass yet filled their casements. Over all rose the keep, a square solid tower, apparently not much injured by wars or weather, and darkened with ivy on one side, wherein wings could be heard flapping uncertainly, as if they belonged to a bird unable to find a proper perch . . . In spite of the habitable and more modern wing, neglect and decay had set their mark upon the outworks of the pile, unfitting them for a more positive light than that of the present hour."

The Yarn Market, Dunster Village

able freely to conjecture from its present appearance what it must have been like two or three centuries back in time.

As I have hinted above, we shall not be able to plod in the footsteps of the actors in this story as we have been able to do in the case of some of the other Wessex Novels, for there is not that exactitude of description regarding the backgrounds which is such a noticeable feature in the majority of the books. For instance, the little hamlet of *Sleeping Green*, where Somerset at first was staying, does not bear sufficient description to warrant us in identifying it with any particular village to be discovered in the immediate neighbourhood of Dunster, though it suggests either Carhampton or Withycombe. *Toneborough*, a barrack town, one may define pretty safely to be an imaginative portrait of Taunton, a town which, in some of the other stories, appears also under the same name. But the description places it some dozen miles nearer to *Stancy Castle* than it actually is.

To return again to *Markton*, or Dunster (called a village sometimes in the novel). It is in the church here – a most interesting one – that the family tombs of the De Stancys are imagined to have stood. The style is mainly that of the fifteenth century, though in the archway of the west door we find a good illustration of Norman work. It stands on the site of an earlier Saxon church, but no tangible evidence of the older fabric is discoverable. A beautifully carved oak screen traverses the entire width of the building, and there are many interesting monuments to be seen. From the belfry the chimes ring out every four hours. On Sunday we may hear *O Rest in the Lord!* On Monday, *Drink to me only!* On Tuesday, *Home, sweet Home!* On Wednesday, *Disposer supreme!* On Thursday, *The Blue Bells of Scotland!* On Friday, *Old 113th!* On Saturday, *Hark, hark, my Soul!* A curious medley of tunes! In the churchyard wall is a wide-arched recess, generally said to mark the site of the stocks, and in the rectory garden may be seen the ruins of a Benedictine Priory.

Close behind the little town is a high hill called Grabhurst, or Grabbist, and from the summit a magnificent bird's-eye view of the surrounding country is obtained. The beautiful Vale of Avill, Dunkery Beacon (scene of the Ballad-tragedy entitled "The Sacrilege," published in *The Fortnightly Review* in 1911), the country from North Hill to Watchet, the Bristol Channel, with Holm Islands standing out strongly, and behind it the line of the Welsh coast, mountains rising back, tier upon tier. Right under our feet clusters the townlet of Dunster, guarded by the castle on one side and Conegar Tower on the other. A huge deer park surrounds the castle, and

Dunster Church *(Markton)*
The site of the tombs of the De Stancys in *A Laodicean*.

through it wanders a sparkling stream.

The few details given above form but a meagre description of the backgrounds of the story, but the present writer fears to stray beyond the bounds of veracity into the realms of imagination.

BIBLIOGRAPHY

Thomas Hardy's England, edited and introduced by John Fowles, with text written by local historian Jo Draper, contains many more photographs by Hermann Lea (Jonathan Cape, 1984). Once again, Lea proves an inspired director of photography (using his live subjects with particular imagination), and the book succeeds as an evocation of life in mid-nineteenth century Dorset despite the fact that the photographs were taken between 1880 and 1910.

Of other guides to Hardy's Wessex two in particular deserve attention. Chronologically they are:

– *The Wessex of Thomas Hardy* by B. C. A. Windle, with illustrations by E. H. New (1902). Windle received topographic advice from Hardy and is sometimes an important authority.

– *The Landscape of Thomas Hardy* by Denys Kay-Robinson, with photographs by Simon McBride (Exeter, 1984). Mr Kay-Robinson has followed in the tracks of Hardy and Lea, and has made numerous interesting discoveries, though occasionally he pops Hardy into a straight-jacket. The actual whereabouts of *Talbothays*, for example – the farm in the Frome Valley where Tess lived for a while – centres on a discussion of Norris Mill Farm being *north*, and Lower Lewell Farm *south*, of the River Frome. It is argued that in the novel *Talbothays* is situated south of the river, therefore the model of *Talbothays* must have been Lower Lewell Farm. This seems to me to ignore the 'ontological' difference between real Dorset and fictional Wessex. Hardy, as the creator of fictional Wessex, had the freedom of a 'literary god' and could put buildings where he wanted them. Thus *Weatherbury Farm* is within half a mile of *Weatherbury*, but Waterston Manor (*Weatherbury Farm*) is a good mile and a half from Puddletown (*Weatherbury*). In any discussions about *Talbothays* some weight should be paid to Hardy's own words (to Clive Holland) that the prototype was Norris Mill Farm. The reader should not be dismayed by the very few 'uncertainties' of identification. In fact they constitute fascinating literary enigmas, perhaps now incapable of final resolution.

The Wessex pilgrim should remember that Hardy was a trained architect. See in particular *Thomas Hardy's Architectural Notebooks* edited by C. J. P. Beatty (Dorchester, 1966). The best life is by Michael Millgate: *Thomas Hardy: A Biography* (Oxford 1982).

The vital source for details about Lea is *Thomas Hardy Through the Camera's Eye*, edited by J. Stevens Cox, Beaminster, 1964; this monograph (no. 20 in the Toucan Press series on the *Life, Times and Works of Thomas Hardy*) includes a memoir about Lea by his nephew A. T. D. Scudamore, Lea's notes for a *Biography of Thomas Hardy*, letters from Lea to Hardy, Lea to Sanders (a Hardy scholar), etc.

Hardy wrote some fifty letters and cards to Lea; these are now preserved in the Sanders collection in the Dorset County Museum, Dorchester; the Oxford University Press series *The Collected Letters of Thomas Hardy* (edited by Professor R. L. Purdy and Professor M. Millgate) will include the texts of this correspondence (see, in particular, volumes 3 and 4, covering the years 1902-1913, O.U.P., 1982, 1984; work still in progress).

For topographical studies of particular novels reference should be made to *The Thomas Hardy Year Book* (Guernsey 1970). See in particular:

– 'The Lower Longpuddle Mystery' by Denys Kay-Robinson (No. 6)

– 'Hermann Lea Reappraised' by Denys Kay-Robinson (No. 6)

Essays on Wessex topography are also to be found in the bulletins of the Thomas Hardy Society (Dorchester, various dates).

PLACE NAME INDEX

Page numbers in italics refer to photographs; italicized words refer to Hardy's names for places.

Thomas Hardy in the Penguin Classics

JUDE THE OBSCURE

A haunting love story, *Jude* is the most outspoken, the most powerful and the most despairing of Thomas Hardy's creations.

FAR FROM THE MADDING CROWD

Perhaps the best-known and most humorous of Hardy's novels, *Far from the Madding Crowd* is the product of his intimate and first-hand knowledge of rural life.

TESS OF THE D'URBERVILLES

Tess is Hardy's most striking and tragic heroine and the character who meant most to him. In a novel full of poetry and mysteriously luminous settings, he unfolds her story with peculiar and unforgettable tenderness and intensity.

THE RETURN OF THE NATIVE

Set in Egdon Heath, whose titanic presence dominates the men and women who live on it, *The Return of the Native*, both powerful and sombre, is sometimes considered the most representative of Hardy's novels.

THE TRUMPET-MAJOR

Light, humorous and observant as it is, *The Trumpet-Major* nevertheless has a vein of tragedy running through it – the unhappiness and despair of unrequited love.

UNDER THE GREENWOOD TREE

The happiest of all Hardy's novels, *Under the Greenwood Tree* formed the foundation of his career as a writer and inaugurated the great series of Wessex novels.

THE MAYOR OF CASTERBRIDGE

A powerful character study of a man whose past refused to be buried, and who is caught by changing conditions of rural commerce.

THE WOODLANDERS

Set in the small community of Little Hintock, on the edge of Blackmoor Vale, *The Woodlanders* catches and holds the lonely courses of individual lives.

THE DISTRACTED PREACHER AND OTHER TALES

These stories are permeated by that atmosphere, narrative power, and vivid sense of place and its intimate relation to character which are the essentials of Hardy's genius.